# From Believing to Knowing

## The Intellectual Certainty of God

RON MACFARLANE

Published 2014 by
Greater Mysteries Publications
Mission, BC, Canada

Cover Design: Ron MacFarlane

Printed in the United States of America

ISBN:
ISBN-13: 978-0994007704
ISBN-10: 0994007701

# DEDICATION

Special thanks to my dear wife, Anne Marie, for her unwavering and enthusiastic support and understanding as I faithfully followed my literary dreams in our precious retirement years.

# CONTENTS

# INTRODUCTION

THERE IS a puzzling and pervasive misconception in present-day thinking that the existence of God cannot be intellectually determined and that mentally accepting the existence of God is strictly a matter of non-rational belief (faith). As such, contemplating God's existence is erroneously regarded as the exclusive subject of faith-based or speculative ideologies (religion and philosophy) which have no proper place in natural scientific study.

The fact is, there are a number of very convincing intellectual arguments concerning the existence of God that have been around for hundreds of years. Indeed, the existence of God can be determined with compelling intellectual certainty—provided the thinker honestly wishes to do so. Moreover, recent advances and discoveries in science have not weakened previous intellectual arguments for God's existence but instead have enormously strengthened and supported them.

Intellectually assenting to the existence of God is easily demonstrated to be a superlatively logical conclusion, not some vague irrational conceptualization. Remarkably, at the present time there are only two seriously competing intellectual explanations of life: the existence of God (the

"God-hypothesis") and the existence of infinite universes (the "multiverse theory"). The postulation of an infinite number of unobservable universes is clearly a desperate attempt by atheistic scientists to avoid the God-hypothesis as the most credible and logical intellectual explanation of life and the universe. Moreover, under intellectual scrutiny, the scientifically celebrated "evolutionary theory" is here demonstrated to be fatally-flawed (philosophically illogical) as a credible explanation of life.

In this particular discourse, five well-known intellectual arguments for God's existence will be thoroughly examined. In considering these arguments, every attempt has been made to include current contributions, advances and discoveries that have modernized the more traditional arguments. Prior to examining these particular arguments for God, the universal predilection to establish intellectual 'oneness'—"monism"—will be considered in detail as well as the recurring propensity to postulate the existence of one supreme being—"monotheism."

Once intellectual certainty of one Supreme Being is established, a number of divine attributes can be logically deduced as well. Eleven of these attributes will be determined and examined in greater detail.

# FROM BELIEVING

# TO KNOWING

# CHAPTER 1

## MONISM: ACKNOWLEDGING THE ONE REALITY

### 1.1 The Intellectual Search for Oneness

"IN THE BEGINNING, before the world of space and time, there was nothing but the sole point of infinity: infinite density, infinite temperature and infinite pressure. Such was the cosmic singularity, the cosmic 'one.' Within the one was all that came to be, all matter and energy in their multitudinous forms.

Alone in eternity, containing all, remained the one. Suddenly, from out of itself, the cosmic unity burst asunder. The light of countless galactic suns rayed forth in all directions. In expanding time and space, the universe and all that is, began—and it was resplendent, majestic and sublime."

What has just been described is not a scriptural passage

1

from an ancient religious manuscript, but a poetic summary of Big Bang cosmogony:[1] the creation of the universe according to contemporary, conventional science.

The notion of a cosmic singularity is a logical inference based on the strong empirical evidence that galaxies are moving away from each other at speeds proportional to their distances. This curious phenomenon was discovered in 1929 by astronomer, Edwin Hubble (1889–1953), and is consequently known as "Hubble's Law." So, if the universe presently appears to be expanding and cooling, perhaps it was once densely compressed and hot at some point in the past. Calculating the current galactic positions and velocities, extrapolating backwards using the equation: velocity = distance/time, scientists are able to determine a point of origin; a single, infinitely-condensed condition termed a "singularity."[2]

There can be, of course, only one original singularity since we know of only one universe that may be collapsible. There have been speculations of a multiverse[3] or parallel universes, but empirically we have no way of knowing what is outside our own universe. Mathematically and observationally, scientists are compelled to accept that there is only one cosmic totality in which we exist. Empirically, the universe is all there is; there is nothing knowable beyond it. Moreover, seeking to understand and explain the one cosmos, scientists further reinforce their position of one reality by establishing 'universals,' laws that apply to all things, everywhere, at all times within the one totality.

Within the recognized cosmos, modern science has also earnestly endeavored to find some kind of ultimate substance, one underlying material from which all things are made. Prior to science, ancient philosophy undertook the first intellectual attempts to solve this existential riddle.

## 1.2 Ancient Greek Philosophical Speculation

In Classical Greece, the philosophical notion that all physical and mental phenomena were derived from a single, fundamental substance was popular and widely accepted. There was, however, diverse opinion as to what that material was. Thales of Miletus (c.625 BC – c.547 BC), for example, believed that the one essential substance of the world was water. Anaximenes (c.546 BC) theorized that everything in nature was comprised of "aer," or 'air,' through a process of rarefaction and condensation (thinning and thickening). To Heraclitus (c.540 BC – 480 BC), it was fire. Thales' pupil, Anaximander (c.611 BC), posited an unknown substance he termed "apeiron" (meaning 'the undefined infinite').

In order to explain the world of observable change, the concept of a fundamental, enduring substance behind all change was logically necessary. Without some factor that persists, all physical activity is merely a succession of unrelated events. Not all Greek philosophers regarded an enduring substrate as a pervasive, homogeneous material. Leucippus (c.500 BC – c.450 BC) and his student Democritus (c.494 BC – c.404 BC) theorized that all observable phenomena was composed of tiny, indivisible particles termed "atomos," meaning 'uncuttable' in Greek. Interestingly, the Nyaya and Vaisheshika schools of philosophy in ancient India had posited a similar idea of 'atoms' one hundred years earlier in the sixth century BC. These schools had even developed elaborate theories of how atoms combined into complex arrangements (first in pairs, then in trios of pairs).

These early philosophical theories of an atomic basis to the physical world were later embraced and cleverly developed by the burgeoning science of chemistry, beginning in 1661 with the British natural philosopher, Robert Boyle (1627–1691). Prior to Boyle, the prevailing theory was Aristotle's contention that, rather than a single underlying material, the physical world was composed of four essentials: earth, water, air and fire. While Aristotle's explanation may seem quaint and simplistic today, if viewed as states of matter rather than as types of material, then viewing all physical phenomena as existing in states of solid (earth), liquid (water), gas (air) or plasma (fire) is remarkably correct.

Matter, according to Boyle, was comprised of tiny particles of varying sizes and shapes that he termed, "corpuscles." Groups and clusters of these tiny corpuscles resulted in an enduring compactness that formed the basic units of chemical and physical processes. Physical properties were determined by changes in shape, size and motion of these corpuscular clusters. Boyle regarded chemical reactions primarily as the association and dissociation of various clusters.

Not surprisingly, in early Greek philosophy, there was no pre-established term for the abstract notion of 'matter.' A similar term, "hyle," was first introduced by Homer (c.800 BC – c.750 BC) and then popularized by Aristotle. Hyle was originally the Greek word for 'timber' or 'lumber;' that is, wood used as a building material. In a broader philosophical sense, then, hyle became the building material of the physical world.

Socrates viewed physical phenomena as the combined result of ideal forms ("morphe") inhering in fundamental matter (hyle), a theory that became known as "hylomorphism." Aristotle was also a strong proponent of hylomorphism, though he rejected the Socratic concept of ideal forms and instead substituted his own idea of substantial and accidental forms. Matter was conceived as being a passive, undifferentiated substance that was shaped by an active principle of essential form.

In intellectually attempting to conceive of a primary principle underlying the physical world, Greek philosophers also employed related terms that have continued to influence current ideas in this area. The term "hypostasis," from the Greek "hypo" ('under') and "hitasthai" ('to stand'), is identical to the English term "substance," from the Latin "sub" ('under') and "stare" ('to stand'). Hypostasis, then, can be understood as the underlying substance of observable reality. The Greek terms "ousia" and "hypokeimenon" are also translated into English as 'substance'; but as noted by Aristotle, both terms can be used to refer to four different kinds of substance: the essence, the universal, the genus and the subject. 'First substance,' the causal agent, was termed by Aristotle "ousia prote"; 'second substance,' the physical effect, he termed "ousia deutera."

The Greek philosophical notion of hyle very seamlessly translates into English as 'matter' since matter is derived from the Latin "materia" which also means 'timber' or 'lumber'; that is, wood used as a raw material or building material. Matter, then, is the basic raw material of the physical world from which all empirical phenomena is formed. Moreover, materia is also associated with the Latin "mater," a term for 'mother.' Matter can therefore be interpreted as the 'mother substance' of reality.

## 1.3  Idealistic Monism

The abstract concept that there is an underlying unity or oneness to the entire world—that 'reality is one,'—can be loosely termed "monism." Monism, as here defined, is not restricted to only postulating a material oneness to reality, which position characterizes "substantial monism' and its subcategories of "neutral monism" and "materialism" (or "physicalism"). Monism can also include intellectual attempts to conceive a metaphysical oneness to reality, which position characterizes "idealism," "phenomenalism" or "mentalistic monism." Rather than the 'all is matter (or energy)' notions of substantial monism, the various theories of idealistic monism maintain that 'all is mind,' that a metaphysical reality of thought and mentation underlies all transient physical phenomena. Idealistic monism can be further distinguished into two subcategories: "objective idealism" and "subjective idealism."

The various theories of objective idealism all share a belief that an all-pervading universal mind is the true reality underlying nature, and is responsible for all physical diversity and change. The most recognized Classical proponent of this philosophical position was, of course, Plato. Plato believed that the physical world of the senses—the realm of appearances—was mutable, transient and therefore unreal. Overshadowing material phenomena, however, were transcendent, enduring supraphysical ideas, universal archetypes, that alone were real.

While clearly advocating a form of universal mind, Plato, like many other objective idealists, recognized an even deeper level of reality with the idea of a supreme being. Not surprisingly, then, many theorists including Plato found it difficult to conceive of an independently existing universal mind without a universal being to possess and employ that mind.

Prior to Plato, the founder of the Eleatic school, Parmenides (c.515 BC – c.450 BC), similarly believed that sensory knowledge was untrustworthy and that reason (mind) alone was reliable. Since sensory change, plurality and origination were unreal, the one reality had to be non-material, immutable and eternal. In the third century, the Neoplatonic philosopher Plotinus also postulated a divine mind ("nous"); but this was an emanation, together with the cosmic soul ("psyche") and the world ("cosmos"), of an absolute being he termed 'the One.' The central doctrine of the Vijnanavada school in fifth century India is a further instance of objective idealism: only consciousness

6

("vijnanamatra") was regarded as real; mind or thought was the ultimate reality, nothing existed outside the mind.

A generalized summary of yoga philosophy regarding universal mind has been presented by Yogi Ramacharaka in *Advanced Course in Yogi Philosophy and Oriental Occultism* (2007):

> The Yogis teach that this Chitta, or mind-substance, is universal and omnipresent—that is, it exists everywhere, and is found at every place in the Universe. Its sum-total is fixed and cannot be added to or taken away from, and therefore it is unchangeable in its sum-total, although like Matter and Energy many apparent changes may occur within itself, resulting from the forming of new combinations.

But again, this universal mind was conceived to be subordinate to a supreme being:

> The Yogis hold that Matter (in itself) does not exist, but is a form of Energy, which Energy is a form of Mind, which Mind is a manifestation of the Absolute. (Ibid)

It has even been suggested that the intellectual notion of 'all is mind' can be traced back to the legendary figure of Hermes Trismegistus in ancient Egypt. In hermetic philosophy, there were seven major principles upon which the entire doctrine was based and the first of these was known as the "principle of mentalism" which stated: "The All is Mind; The Universe is Mental." As explained in *The Kybalion: A Study of the Hermetic Philosophy of Ancient Egypt and Greece* (2007):

> This Principle embodies the truth that "All is Mind." It explains that The All (which is the Substantial Reality underlying all outward manifestations and appearances which we know under the terms of "The Material Universe"; and "Phenomena of Life"; "Matter"; "Energy"; and, in short, all that is apparent to our material senses) ...

may be considered and thought of as an Universal, Infinite, Living Mind.

Throughout later European history, various thinkers continued to theorize of an objective mental oneness to reality. Interestingly, in the twentieth century this philosophical notion was embraced and supported more by natural scientists than by modern philosophers. Noted British astrophysicist, Arthur Eddington (1882–1944), for example, even more succinctly than Plato, wrote: "The stuff of the world is mind-stuff." To clarify that he meant objective, universal mind-stuff, Eddington added:

> The mind-stuff of the world is, of course, something more general than our individual conscious minds; but we may think of its nature as not altogether foreign to the feelings in our consciousness." (*The Nature of the Physical World*, 1935)

Fellow Cambridge physicist and astronomer, James Jeans (1877–1946), strongly echoed Eddington's mental monism in his book, *The Mysterious Universe* (2011):

> [T]he universe can best be pictured, although still very imperfectly and inadequately, as consisting of pure thought, the thought of what, for want of a wider word, we must describe as a mathematical thinker. If the universe is a universe of thought, then its creation must have been an act of thought ... substantial matter resolving itself into a creation and manifestation of mind.

Most modern-day idealist philosophers, beginning with Rene Descartes (1596–1650), conceived that the one reality was determined by the subjective mental activity of individual human beings rather than by an objective, all-pervasive mental activity underpinning the entire universe. For them, the belief, 'all is mind,' was better expressed as, "all that we know is entirely the product of our own minds." This particular monist worldview has therefore been termed, "subjective idealism." Numerous variations of subjective idealism have been propounded by philosophers such as Immanuel Kant (1724–1804), Johann Gottlieb Fichte (1762–1814), G.W.F. Hegel (1770–1831), Arthur Schopenhauer (1788–1860) and George Berkeley (1685–1753).

This particular philosophical doctrine is perhaps best summarized by Kant in *Critique of Pure Reason* (1996):

> [I]f I remove the thinking subject, the whole material world must at once vanish because it is nothing but a phenomenal appearance in the sensibility of ourselves as a subject, and a manner or species of representation … In the true sense of the word, therefore, I can never perceive external things, but I can only infer their existence from my own internal perception.

It should be clear from the entire foregoing discourse on monism, that philosophers and scientists since the dawn of the Intellectual Age have been overwhelmingly impelled to postulate a oneness to reality. Why this is so, is open to conjecture, but one obvious explanation is that reality empirically compels us to do so. The repeated observations of our physical senses throughout time have thus far revealed only one universe. A further explanation is that we also appear to be motivated by our own psychology, what has been described as a 'metaphysical inclination for unity.'[4] Establishing harmony where there is disharmony, unity where there is disunity, can be very psychologically satisfying, both intellectually and emotionally. The scientific search for a 'theory of everything' which would unite the disparate theories of gravity, electromagnetism and the strong and weak nuclear forces, is one such example of this metaphysical, psychological motivation.

One would obviously expect to find a similarly powerful

unificatory impetus among theologians and religious thinkers throughout history as well.

# CHAPTER 2

# MONOTHEISM: REALITY AS ONE UNIVERSAL BEING

## 2.1 Principal Variations of Monotheism

WHEN THE ONE reality is intellectually conceived to be a single supernatural being or deity, then monism morphs into monotheism (from the Greek for 'one god'). Moreover, the broad concept of monotheism can be further refracted into a number of differing secondary concepts, due primarily to the distinction of God and the universe (creator and creation, theos and cosmos) and the consequent relationship between the two. The principal variations of monotheism are listed and briefly described as follows:

(1) "Deism": the belief in an undefined god, based on reason rather than revelation, who is transcendent and who does not intervene in the created universe once it has been established.

(2) "Theism": the belief in a personal god, a supreme being, who created the universe and who spiritually extends beyond it; but who also remains involved in the universe,

11

such as in human affairs.

(3) "Pantheism": the belief that the universe itself is God, who is not transcendent or extraneous to it. There is no distinction of creator and creation; God and nature are merely two names for the same reality.

(4) "Monistic theism": the belief in a supreme being in which there is a plurality of created souls. The universe is a temporary illusion (maya); the only reality is God, the Absolute.

(5) "Henotheism": maintains devotion to a supreme god without denying the existence of other gods. "Kathenotheism" ("serial henotheism") is the worship of a succession of gods but only one at a time.

(6) "Monolatrism": maintains that only one god deserves to be worshipped among many other gods due to a special relationship which this deity has with the worshippers.

(7) "Panentheism": the belief that the one God is both immanent and transcendent in association with the created universe. God pervades the universe but is not identical to it—the universe is contained within God.

(8) "Substance monotheism": the belief that there exists many gods but that they are all just different forms of a single underlying spiritual substance.

## 2.2   A Brief History of Monotheism

Interestingly, the conceptualization of some form of monotheistic worldview began to unfold at the nascency of the Intellectual Age around 3000 BC. The first recorded public declaration of monotheistic belief was in ancient Egypt by the pharaoh, Akhenaten (c.1385 BC – c.1350 BC). Akhenaten rejected belief in Egypt's numerous gods, including the primary, traditional deity, Amun-Re, and instead instituted the exclusive worship of Aten, the sun god, as the only true god.

Sometime later, during the reign of King Josiah, around 621 BC, the monotheistic worship of Yahweh became dominant among the ancient Hebrews. Prior to this time, the common pre-intellectual worship of multiple gods—polytheism—was the dominant Hebrew form of religion. The neopythagorean philosophers, such as Apollonius of Tyana (c.40 AD–c.120 AD), monotheistically postulated an ultimate One they termed "the Monad." Neoplatonism adhered to the idea of an effable, transcendent God, 'the One,' who emanated the divine mind ("nous"), the cosmic soul ("psyche") and the world ("cosmos").

In ancient India, the monotheistic notion of universal oneness was described in the Nasadiya Sukta of the *Rig Veda* as the one being/non-being who "breathed without breath." According to the Advaita Vedanta as expounded by Shankara (c.788–c.820), "All is Brahma": the divine, formless, ineffable ground of all being. Many other schools of Hindu philosophy held to subtle variations of monotheism, such as panentheism and monistic theism.

By maintaining that the ultimate nature of the universe is a transcendent emptiness, termed "nirvana," some schools of Buddhist philosophy, such as Mahayana and Theravada Buddhism, can also be regarded as religiously monist, though not necessarily monotheist as commonly understood.

Chapter 112 of the Qur'an succinctly expresses the Islamic monotheistic belief regarding one supreme deity:

Say, he is God the one, God the eternal. He does not beget nor was he begotten, and there is nothing that is like him [or] equal to him.

While monist concerning God, orthodox Islamic belief does not consider the Creator and the created world as equal, claiming that God created the universe from nothing.

Rather remarkably, Christianity (in all its forms) has in

only two thousand years grown from a tiny persecuted sect in the Mediterranean and Middle East, into a worldwide religious force. Of the 7.280 billion people in the world today (2014), 2.1 billion profess to be Christian—almost one-third of the world's population. Needless to say, the monotheistic worldview of Christianity has had a major influence on all aspects of world culture and has paralleled the development of intellectual thought. In many respects, the spread of Christianity has acted as a counter-weight (some would say, counter-brake) to scientific development.

While there has certainly been dualistic and pluralistic thought systems developed throughout recorded history, some unitary conception of the universe, some form of monism, has overwhelmingly dominated the Intellectual Age right up to the present day. Even seemingly dualistic or pluralistic worldviews have strong elements of monism. Ancient Persian Zoroastrianism, for instance, is often cited as a prime example of a dualistic worldview. Cosmic dualism, according to this belief system, arose from the opposing actions of two co-equal, co-powerful and co-eternal supernatural deities: the lord of goodness and light, Ahura Mazda (also known as Ormuzd), and the opposing lord of evil and darkness, Angra Mainyu (or Ahriman). All that existed and occurred in the known world was the result of this bitheistic opposition.

However, since worship was ultimately directed to Ahura Mazda, Zoroastrianism clearly included strong monotheistic elements, particularly in the area of henotheism. In the *Gathas,* for example, the only divinity recognized or mentioned by name is Ahura Mazda. While other "Ahuras" ('Lords') were generally acknowledged, Ahura Mazda was addressed as "thou who art the mightiest Ahura and the Wise One." (Yasna 33.11) Furthermore, a no-longer practiced branch of Zoroastrianism, known as Zurvanism, monotheistically included a single creator god called Zurvan

Akarana ('Infinite Space-Time') who was the primordial father god to the rival brother gods, Ahura Mazda and Angra Mainyu.

## 2.3   Mankind's Pre-Intellectual 'Oneness'

At this point, the question naturally arises, "Why weren't monistic worldviews conceived during mankind's extensive pre-intellectual (prehistoric) past?" The obvious reason is that in the early stages of ancestral cognitive evolution, the complex abstract intellection needed to formulate a thought conception of the universe (a worldview) was not developmentally possible. Moreover, primordial mankind had not yet unfolded the psychological conditions necessary for independent objective thought—particularly a clear subject-object distinction—that is, the ability to separate self from the environment.

Pre-intellectual humans had no need to establish a conceptual unity, to rationally formulate a universal oneness, since they already felt and experienced an instinctive oneness with all-embracing nature. By directly perceiving themselves as intimately connected to the diverse environment around them, our pre-intellectual ancestors correspondingly developed an animistic and polytheistic spiritual relationship with nature. For them, human experience was an inseparable blending of the supernatural with the natural, of the otherworldly with the worldly.

From the early emergence of conscious awareness to the present day, then, humanity has been predisposed to experiential unity, to existential oneness. At first this unity was dimly perceived and experienced as a child-like oneness with the natural environment. By degrees (over thousands of years), as the individualized self psychologically separated out of this experiential unity, the perception of a distinct physical world likewise crystallized to a lower level of awareness while the distillated awareness of pure spirit ascended to a higher conscious level.

Humanity, still in the afterglow of the original, instinctive spiritual oneness, now viewed reality in terms of heaven and earth, Creator and creation, God and the universe. Through prolonged psychological separation, the spirit world and the physical world grew cold to each other in mankind's experience. The innate sense of oneness, the lost warmth of primordial unity, was kept aglow throughout the Intellectual Age by monistic conceptualization (theologically, philosophically and scientifically); that is, by attempting to establish an enduring unified worldview in the human mind.

Prior to the Intellectual Age, then, universal oneness was experienced not conceived. The abstract notion of a transcendent reality, God, would not have been intellectually formulated. The protean interweaving of spirit and matter was experienced as a rich diversity of spiritual beings and life in nature. Early mankind's vague sense of self extended outwardly to all that was perceived. The reality of one universal being, one all-pervading self, was not a mental conception but a deep, inborn, unconceived, personally-experienced feeling.[5]

Now that humanity possesses the intellectual capacity to abstractly conceptualize the phenomenal world in terms of spirit and matter, Creator and creation, God and the universe, what does reason and logical thinking have to say about the idea of God? Is there any truth to this idea, any grounding in reality?

# CHAPTER 3

# PROVING GOD: CONCEIVING THE INCONCEIVABLE?

## 3.1 Modern Science Affirms the Supraphysical and the Supernatural

FROM THE FOREGOING analyses of monism and monotheism, the significant conclusion (perhaps surprising to some) is that scientists, theologians, philosophers and everyday thinkers all overwhelmingly share a common belief in one reality. They differ, as we have seen, as to the fundamental nature of that single reality: is it universal matter (and/or energy), universal mind or universal spirit (God)?

But here again, the widely supported cosmogony of modern science and the origin beliefs of current monotheistic religions are rapidly moving closer together, much closer than many of us realize. It is astounding to discover that today scientists and theologians now share the notion that our universe of matter and energy began as a supernatural event outside space and time! Theologians term this cosmogenetic oneness, God; scientists term it the cosmic or Big Bang

17

singularity. Once again, not surprisingly, there are striking differences between science and religion as to the fundamental nature of this pre-universal unity.

It is a commonly-held misconception, particularly among scientists, that natural science does not acknowledge or recognize the non-material or the supernatural. But with the formulation of Big Bang theory, now both of these assertions are no longer correct. For instance, energy (in its multiple forms) is non-material in the sense that it does not have mass and it cannot be observed directly using the five physical senses, only indirectly by its effects on matter; that is, by its ability to do work or to cause motion. According to Einsteinian relativity, however, energy is interconvertible with matter; but as energy, it is by definition, not matter, non-material.

Moreover, mathematics, that indispensable tool in the workshop of empirical science, is an abstract product of the human mind and is, therefore, non-material. Ideas do not exist in three-dimensional space. The brain, of course, is made of matter and thinking activity in the brain will generate chemical and electromagnetic activity; but at no time has science been able to tangibly weigh, measure or observe a discrete, isolated mathematical idea under a microscope.

Physical science, then, does acknowledge and recognize non-material aspects of the universe. So, what about the supernatural? Once again, the popular notion, even amongst scientists, is that hard science automatically rejects anything of a supernatural character as either non-existent or outside the range of physical science. But all that changed with the development of Big Bang theory.

## 3.2: The Big Bang Singularity

The scientific notion that the universe had some sort of

beginning, that it was not infinite in time, was soon recognized as a mathematical consequence of Einstein's general theory of relativity (1915–1916). The unavoidable calculation of a finite cosmological beginning was at first resisted by many prominent scientists, including Arthur Eddington, who stated, "Philosophically, the notion of a beginning to the present order is repugnant to me and I should like to find a genuine loophole." Even Einstein himself attempted to avoid this consequence of his own theory by introducing a cosmological constant, a mathematical 'fudge factor' that would continue to yield a static model of the universe. Later regretting this attempt, Einstein grudgingly accepted what he called "the necessity for a beginning."

The necessity for a cosmic beginning was the logical inference of relativity calculations first introduced in 1922 by mathematician, Alexander Friedman (1888–1925), that indicated the universe was not static but expanding. A universe that was moving apart clearly implied a point in time when this movement began.

The idea that a 'creation-like' event must have occurred in the history of the universe was first proposed in *Nature* (1931) by Belgian astrophysicist and Catholic priest, Georges Lemaitre (1894–1966). Lemaitre termed this initial point of expansion the "Primeval Atom" and also referred to it as "the Cosmic Egg exploding at the moment of creation." The now-familiar term, "Big Bang," was initially used in 1950 as a sarcastic designation by British astronomer, Fred Hoyle (1915–2001), since he was not a strong supporter of Lemaitre's theory.

In 1946, Russian-born scientist George Gamow (1904–1968) theorized that the Big Bang began as a concentration of pure energy, a primeval fireball that was the source of all matter and energy in the universe which suddenly exploded outwardly into numerous expanding galaxies. This idea of an initial, cataclysmic Big Bang explosion was later modified and understood to be more in the nature of a rapid, balloon-like expansion instead.

Between 1968 and 1970, Big Bang theory was given substantial support and clarification with the formulation of the "singularity theorem" by three British astrophysicists, Stephen Hawking (b.1942), George Ellis (b.1939) and Roger Penrose (b.1931). Their theorem mathematically demonstrated that every solution to the equations of general relativity guaranteed the existence of a singular boundary for space and time in the distant past. By extrapolating backward to hypothetical time = 0, the result was a universe of size = 0. According to their calculations, then, time and space had a finite beginning that also corresponded to the origin of matter and energy. The Big Bang singularity didn't appear at a certain spot in space at a particular point in time; but rather, it created space and time itself upon expansion. Prior to the singularity, nothing of the known universe existed: no matter, energy, space or time. The infinitesimal singularity appeared out of nowhere from causes unknown.

As it stands now, the Big Bang singularity of cosmic origin is understood as a cosmological point of zero volume, with infinite density and infinite temperature. Moreover, at the point of singularity, the curvature of space-time is also infinite which means that the general theory of relativity ceases to apply. As Hawking has written, "the actual point of creation, the singularity, is outside the scope of presently known laws of physics"; (*The Large-Scale Structure of Space-Time*; 1973) and "In real time, the universe has a beginning and an end at singularities [black holes][6] that form a boundary to space-time and at which the laws of science breaks down." (*A Brief History of Time*; 1998)

Since the cosmological singularity and black hole singularities are points at which the laws of science no longer apply, what is shattering for scientific materialism is that not only was there a time (currently calculated at 13.7 billion years ago) when the physical universe of matter, energy, space and time did not exist; but prior to the birth of the universe there existed a singularity that was 'supernatural,' that was outside the known laws of physical nature.

Whether the Big Bang theory continues to hold true in the future or whether the universe actually began as a singularity, the significant fact remains that modern physical science does indeed seriously consider select notions concerning the supraphysical and the supernatural.

Since scientific cosmogony and monotheistic religion both conceive the universe as occurring before time out of a supraphysical oneness, the notion of a supernatural creator should no longer appear quite so scientifically foreign or unreasonable. As Hawking has stated: "So long as the universe had a beginning, we could suppose it had a creator." (*A Brief History of Time*) Though a single, supernatural origin to the universe does not, of course, equate to God, what is it about a monotheistic conception of origin that remains difficult for many scientific thinkers to accept?

## 3.3   Scientific Objections to Theistic Universal Creation

One basic, recurring scientific objection is that a non-physical creator cannot be empirically validated; that is, it can't be observed with the five physical senses and tested with the recognized methods of physical science. A second fundamental scientific objection is that while there are numerous conflicting conceptions of a creator-God, all conceptions include the characteristics of all-being, all-life, all-consciousness, all-intelligence and all-goodness. Present-day natural science cannot conceive of any such discarnate qualities underlying the physical universe. According to science: being, life, consciousness, intelligence and morality are all transitory effects of human existence that have no separate reality apart from the human body and therefore do not exist prior to birth or after death.

The first-mentioned scientific objection that a non-material, cosmic origin is beyond the ability of physical science to know can be countered by once again recalling the scientific study of energy in all its forms. Science is unable to observe energy directly but only indirectly through its effects on matter. Moreover, the presence and behaviour of energy can be predicted or inferred prior to the observation of its effects by using mathematical calculation. In this case, the non-material cause (energy) is understood through its material effects (movement of matter).

Effects, then, are extensions or reflections of the cause. A specific example is the action of magnetic energy on a scattering of iron filings: knowledge of the nature of magnetism, such as magnetic fields and polarity, is inferred by observing the uniquely patterned effects of the iron filings. By the same logic, if the universe has a supersensible creator, then knowledge of that creator-cause can be inferred by studying the created universe-effect. If some of the characteristics of a supernatural singularity can be scientifically deduced from the constitution and behaviour of the physical universe, then characteristics of a supernatural creator-cause can be similarly deduced from the observational study of the physical universe. Logically concluding, it is therefore scientifically possible to acquire knowledge of a supernatural creator, providing of course that such a creator exists.

The second, nettlesome scientific objection to a monotheistic conception of cosmogenesis is that the term, "God," as it is commonly understood by religion and theology, really means 'personal God' or 'Supreme Being.' If God only referred to a single, unitary, supernatural condition out of which the entire universe arose, then natural science would have no objection to the term. God could mean the Big Bang singularity. Or similarly, as theorized by physicist and mathematician, Frank Tipler (b.1947), the universe may eventually cease expanding and undergo a cosmic collapse, a "Big Crunch," resulting in an end-time singularity he termed "the Omega Point." Tipler identifies this Omega Point as God. Though a Big Crunch scenario has not been supported by recent astronomical observations, Tipler's Omega Point theory demonstrates that the term, God, can be used in a scientific sense when it is used impersonally, without any personal characteristics of life and being. But for the vast majority of monotheistic believers, it is not possible to strip the definition of God of the essential characteristics of life and being and still mean God.

## 3.4    The Logical Necessity of a Supernatural Creator-Being

The Dutch philosopher, Baruch Spinoza (1632–1677), is quoted as stating: "And we must remember that every people make their God in their own image. A man's God is himself at his best; his devil is himself at his worst." This statement has often been negatively understood to mean that God and the devil are only inventions of the human mind and therefore have no objective reality. However, Spinoza's quotation can also be positively understood to mean that, in the case of God, any conception of an ultimate creator of the universe must also include the entirety of what makes us human: life, consciousness, being and morality. If these qualities exist in us then they exist in the universe; and if the universe was created by God (and God is all there is) then these qualities must logically exist in God as well. Where else could they have come from? The same rationale is used with the Big Bang singularity: all matter, energy, space and time—everything in the physical universe must be contained in this point of origin. Where else could they have come from?

In monotheism, the human qualities of being, life, consciousness and morality are logically extended to an absolute degree since God is conceived as the one and only, outside of which there is nothing else, and therefore without exterior addition. These qualities, then, are conceived as supreme being, all life, total consciousness and perfect goodness. Conceiving the creator-God as an ultimate extension of intrinsic human characteristics, then, is not an irrational or delusional endeavour but quite a logical thing to do.

Likewise assigning the characteristics of being, life, consciousness and morality to a supraphysical source is also quite understandable and reasonable given that physical science does not adequately explain these things from its material perspective. Seen in all its unvarnished ideological glory, the uncompromising materialism of physical science has attempted to reduce the wonders and richness of human life: art, literature, music, society, relationships, technology, thoughts, dreams, feelings, willing, creating, even mathematics and science itself as being the accidental by-products of a temporary, purposeless assemblage of nuclear particles. The human being is simply regarded as a temporal material form, a body of physical matter and energy, a unique chemical accident in an otherwise lifeless universe without meaning or purpose. The psychological features of being, consciousness and morality are seen as the electrical discharges and chemical secretions of a physical brain[7] that quickly deteriorates in accordance with the law of entropy. "Life" is simply the term used to describe the short-term activity of lifeless molecules when they are arranged into specific complex forms. As expressed by neurologist, V. S. Ramachandran (b.1952), in *A Brief Tour of Human Consciousness:*

*from Imposter Poodles to Purple Numbers* (2004):

> Even though it is common knowledge, it never ceases to amaze me that all the richness of our mental life—all our feelings, our emotions, our thoughts, our ambitions, our love lives, our religious sentiments and even what each of us regards as his or her intimate private self—is simply the activities of these little specks of jelly in our heads, in our brains. There is nothing else.

According to physical science, then, there is nothing particularly special about being, consciousness or morality. They are nothing more than isolated examples of chemical activity in a vast, cosmic sea awash with molecular activity. Life is just a degree of chemical complexity; and of course life has no purpose because it is only a physical effect in a purposeless universe.

Not surprisingly, while this dreary reductionism is the official conceptual framework on which the entire edifice of physical science today stands, no scientist or scientific supporter actually directs his or her life in accordance with this impossible worldview. As human beings, we all strive for purpose in our lives, to find meaning in our existence. Science itself 'searches for the truth,' 'strives to solve the riddles of the universe,' 'endeavours to find cures for human affliction' and 'attempts to solve the problems of human society.' If we are all concerned with purpose, but purpose cannot arise from a purposeless universe, then that only logically leaves a supraphysical source for this impulse in our lives.

No scientific thinker behaves as if he or she is a directionless, chemically-driven machine—a complete physical automaton—without conscious awareness, without a sense of self, without a feeling of being alive and without a concern for right and wrong. No scientific thinker behaves as if he or she has no independent ability to choose and is blindly driven about by the chemical forces in their brain.

Moreover, physical scientists don't behave as if life on earth was merely a humdrum effect of otherwise ordinary and universal chemistry. If there is nothing chemically special about life, why strive to enhance it, or help it or prolong it? If all the noblest features of life, including our sense of self, are nothing but brain jelly, why do scientists themselves worry about and attempt to avoid dying? Why is our little blue planet the only place in this cosmic expanse of galaxies, nebulae, suns and planets that has physical life if there is nothing out-of-the-ordinary about life?

Despite the minimizing effects of the natural scientific worldview, few intelligent thinkers are not filled with wonder, awe and amazement at the experience of being alive and the thrill of being conscious of oneself and the surrounding universe. No amount of physical brain research[8] can circumvent the scientific worldview that the entire material substratum of the universe and every single nuclear particle and quantum of energy is lifeless, without purpose, devoid of consciousness and incapable of self-awareness. So, if the wondrous features of existence are not the result of molecular brain matter, then they must be the result of supraphysical causation. Once again, it is not logically unreasonable or irrational to consider the possibility of a supernatural creator-being to the cosmos.

Scientifically, then, the human being in relationship to the rest of the universe is like a 'god in the machine': an anomalous creator-being filled with life; conscious of itself and its surroundings; capable of thought, feeling and willing; directing its behavior according to principles of morality, fairness, justice and purpose, while the rest of the material universe, in all its beauty and splendor, mechanically moves with blind, inerrant chemical precision. In contrast, the rational religious reconciliation of this cosmic disparity was to regard mankind (as did the ancient Hebrews) as being created in "the image and likeness of God"—the microcosmic creation of a supernatural, macrocosmic creator.

From the foregoing discourse, then, intellectually considering the existence of a personal God, a living, supraphysical creator-being instead of an undefined, impersonal condition of primal unity beyond the boundaries of natural law, is a reasonable explanation for the unique phenomena of life—particularly human life—especially given the limitations of scientific understanding. Given the reasonableness of such an idea, is it possible to offer rational proof for the existence of a monotheistic creator?

## 3.5  The Basis of Proof for a Monotheistic Creator

Unfortunately, addressing this important question very much depends on what the enquirer is willing to accept as proof and, of course, what is the understanding of God that is being examined (since there are varying conceptions). If, for instance, God is conceived as a large, aged, grey-bearded monarch sitting on a massive throne somewhere up in heaven meting out divine justice by rewarding his followers and punishing his enemies, then this Old Testament-style idea can be easily dismissed. If God is conceived as a transcendent, supraphysical intelligence that invisibly underlies the substance, organization and activity of the visible universe, then this conception will obviously require a deeper level of ratiocination. As expressed by American astronomer, Carl Sagan (1934–1996):

> The idea that God is an oversized white male with a flowing beard, who sits in the sky and tallies the fall of every sparrow, is ludicrous. But if by 'God' one means the set of physical laws that govern the universe, then clearly there is such a God.

Very often, atheistically-inclined thinkers refute the idea of a monotheistic being by using 'straw man' argumentation; that is, using the fallacy of extension. This deceptive technique establishes an exaggerated or caricatured concept of God, a straw man, and then intellectually knocks it over, thereby claiming to disprove the existence of God. The 'Guy Upstairs' is certainly a common term for God and Michelangelo's Sistine Chapel does indeed depict God as an athletic, grey-bearded European male; but these are not the only and certainly not the most intellectually demanding ideas of God that have been historically conceived throughout the world.

As to the degree of proof that is acceptable, many serious thinkers conclude that the visible universe is proof enough of God's existence; that the beauty, order, majesty, diversity, grandeur and complexity of the perceived universe is undoubtedly the handiwork of a supreme, intelligent being. Albert Einstein in many respects typifies this viewpoint:

> I am satisfied with the mystery of the eternity of life and with the awareness and a glimpse of the marvelous structure of the existing world, together with the devoted striving to comprehend a portion, be it ever so tiny, of the Reason that manifests itself in nature. (*The World As I See It*; 2007)

Other thinkers are more skeptically hardened. Similar to Thomas, the doubting apostle of the risen Christ, the uncompromising attitude of these thinkers is that only by physically 'touching' God is there convincing proof. The dedicated materialist will only be empirically satisfied when God can be weighed, measured and boiled in a beaker; for them, anything less is a waste of time.

Nevertheless, despite the wide range of disagreement as to what constitutes acceptable proof, rational arguments for the existence of God are not new; but rather, have been proposed and widely debated by philosophers and theologians for hundreds of years. Muslim philosopher, Ibn Sina (966–1037), is acknowledged as the originator of what became known later as the ontological and cosmological arguments for the existence of God, which he postulated in the "Metaphysics" section of the *Book of Healing*. A more well-known ontological argument was later proposed by Anselm of Canterbury (1033–1109) in the second chapter of *Proslogion*.

Undoubtedly, the most famous historical attempt to rationally demonstrate the existence of God was by St. Thomas Aquinas in *Summa Theologica* (1265–1274). The five logical proofs of God advanced by Aquinas and later Scholastic thinkers demonstrated the Catholic Church's position, then and now, that God exists and can be rationally known without recourse to claims of revelation. As declared by Pius X (1835–1914): "Deum … natural: rationis lumine per ea quae facta sunt, hoc est per visibilia creationis opera, tanquam causam per effectus certo cognosci adeoque demostrari etiam posse, profiteor" ("I declare that by the natural light of reason, God can be certainly known and therefore his existence demonstrated through the things that are made, that is, through the visible works of creation, as the cause is known through its effects"). The Church does not claim, however, that God's existence can be proven or demonstrated in a mathematical way, as a proposition in geometry is proven, merely that God can be intellectually "known with certainty."

Many other religious denominations share this position, a fact that contradicts the popular misconception that all faith-based institutions believe that the existence of God must be accepted entirely on the basis of blind faith without any appeal to logic and reason.

## 3.6  Five Traditional Arguments for God's Existence

Most traditional arguments fall into five main conceptual categories that continue to be acknowledged, developed and passionately debated even today. They are listed and concisely described as follows:

(1) The ontological argument: If human beings are able to formulate ideas of God (to have God consciousness), then that implies the existence of a God who instilled such a conscious possibility.

(2) The cosmological argument: If the majestic expanse of the universe had a beginning, then it is fundamentally an effect and therefore requires a superior cause; that is, God.

(3) The teleological argument: If the universe inherently exhibits the characteristics of design, then it must have a purpose or direction and therefore a grand designer; that is, God.

(4) The rational argument: If the universe operates according to order and natural law, then it must have a comprehensive mind underlying it; that is, the mind of God.

(5) The moral argument: If human behaviour is directed by principles of right and wrong, then this innate moral consciousness has to be infused by a higher moral being; that is, God.

In order to appreciate the depth and complexity of these five arguments for God's existence, each will be examined in more detail with a view to including any recent developments in philosophy and natural science as well as relevant esoteric and mystical knowledge and the research of spiritual science (anthroposophy).

# CHAPTER 4

# THE ONTOLOGICAL ARGUMENT FOR GOD'S EXISTENCE

## 4.1 The Basic Argument

THE ONTOLOGICAL ARGUMENT, in its simplest form: 'If we can conceive of God then he must exist,' is strictly an a priori proof that relies on logic and reason alone without any appeal to observation. Many philosophers, including David Hume and Immanuel Kant, as well as the Catholic Church, find this basic ontological argument unconvincing since the premise relies on the conclusion which in turn relies on the premise. In its most divested form, then, the ontological argument can be regarded as a circular argument, a bare assertion fallacy that offers no supporting premise other than qualities inherent to the unproven statement.

There are, however, more sophisticated modern versions of the ontological argument that are not as easy to refute. The complex example proposed by American philosopher, Alvin Plantinga (b.1932), can be summarized as a logically valid syllogism:

1. By definition, if it is possible that God exists, then
2. It is possible that God exists
3. Therefore, God exists

Applying this argument, to logically deny that God exists, one must prove that it is impossible for God to exist. While it may be difficult to logically prove that God exists, it is equally difficult to prove that God does not exist as well.

Considering the predilection of the human mind to conceive of God, while it is certainly true that not every fleeting thought that passes through the human mind corresponds to an objective reality, in the case of the monotheistic concept of a personal God, the fact that so many people for so long have so fervently and so strongly entertained this notion does reasonably suggest that there must be some truth to it. Otherwise, why would so many people be willing to delude themselves, for so long, if there was no reality to this idea?

A similar line of reasoning can be used regarding the historical reality of Jesus who, some claim due to scant historical evidence, never existed. Once again, why would almost one-third of the world's population continue to affirm this belief if there was no truth to it?

Admittedly, people can be incredibly gullible on a grand scale and can certainly hold onto incorrect notions for long periods of time (the idea of a flat earth, for example); but the persevering belief in the existence of God is not easily explained away. The fact that a great many people have found comfort and solace in a belief in God does not necessarily mean that the idea is an imaginary, psychological placebo. The fact that believing in God has, for billions of people, provided satisfying answers to deep, troubling and complex questions about existence does not necessarily mean that the idea is a superficial mental crutch that supports faulty reasoning. The fact that believing in God places greater emphasis on moral behaviour does not necessarily mean that broad acceptance is coerced from fear of damnation, hellfire or divine retribution. The fact that believers place a degree of trust and faith in a Supreme Being who is incomprehensively greater than the entire universe, does not necessarily mean that the idea of God is perpetuated by blind, irrational acquiescence.

## 4.2 The Weakness of Science to Explain 'Being' (Self-Consciousness)

While various versions of the ontological argument are clearly weak as conclusive proof of God's existence, at best they demonstrate that belief in God is no less rational than disbelief. Moreover, the overall ontological argument still challenges the modern materialistic worldview by raising the question: "How is it that 'being' (the focus of ontology), defined in this case as 'self-conscious awareness,' can arise entirely from the matter and energy constitution of the human body?"

Since matter in all its forms from nuclear particles to various energies is, according to natural science, entirely insensate—completely and utterly devoid of consciousness, feeling and volition—how is it that humans are not only aware of their surroundings but are aware of themselves as unique entities, as individualized centres of consciousness? Modern attempts to explain consciousness and self-awareness as products of brain activity are unsound and futile since a material brain, of itself, is nothing but matter and energy. Expressed as a logical syllogism:

1. Scientifically, matter and energy are entirely insensate
2. The human brain is composed exclusively of matter and energy
3. Therefore, the brain is insensate

If 'beingness' (self-conscious awareness) does not arise from the physical universe, then logically it must arise from a supraphysical source. Just as every distinct particle of matter is scientifically calculated to have a single, supernatural point of origin in the Big Bang singularity, so every separate entity of self-conscious awareness, every human being, can be postulated to have a single, supernatural point of origin in a supreme being, that is, God.

Rather than the traditional ontological argument of 'I conceive God, therefore God is,' an alternative argument can also be formulated as, 'I am, therefore God is.' Human self-awareness is succinctly expressed in the words, 'I am.' Rather interestingly, in Exodus 2:13, when Moses asks God for his divine name, God declares that it is simply, "I AM." From this scriptural passage, the ancient Hebrews clearly understood God as a being who is self-aware. No doubt it would be inconceivable then, as it is now, that human beings possessed the ability to be self-aware, but that God did not. Human self-awareness is possible, then, because God, the ultimate source of consciousness, is self-aware. In other words, declaring 'I am' is humanly possible because 'God is.'

## 4.3 The Mystical Version of the Ontological Argument

A deeper, more mystical version of the ontological argument of 'I am, therefore God is,' can be used to offer more compelling proof of God's existence. Normally the assertion, 'I am,' simply denotes self-awareness, the conscious recognition of a personal self that is separate and distinct from the rest of the world. This everyday self is further associated with individual thoughts, feelings, memories, likes, dislikes, family relations, bodily characteristics, national ties, friends, names and so on. At this level of awareness, since the self is identified with personal associations that change, the ego is perceived to be a transitory self that is subject to birth, becoming, growth, maturation, waking, sleeping, decline and death. One's self, the 'I,' is not perceived as permanent, but ever changing. As expressed by Armenian mystic, G. I. Gurdjieff:

> Man such as we know him, the 'man-machine,' ... cannot have a permanent and single I. His I changes as quickly as his thoughts, feelings and moods, and he makes a profound mistake in considering himself always one and the same person; in reality he is always a different person, not the one he was a moment ago. (P. D. Ouspensky; *In Search of the Miraculous: Fragments of an Unknown Teaching*; 1947)

At a deeper level of awareness, however, the I is subjectively perceived to have a permanent, unchangeable quality. Even though thoughts, feelings, surroundings and circumstances my change, the subject—the centre of consciousness who experiences the vicissitudes of internal and external change—remains the same. One's I cannot become someone else's I; it is always the same I throughout one's entire life, no matter what the transitory situation. The realization that the I has an enduring quality over time can be termed 'soul consciousness' as distinct from 'self consciousness.'

Processes of initiation can lead to an even further deepening of self-awareness to the point of experiencing the mystical realization that the true self transcends the body and the mind. The I now inwardly experiences and knows with certainty ("gnosis") that it is 'spirit': eternal, alive, aware and real. When the higher self declares, 'I AM,' it is affirming, in truth, its spiritual reality and oneness with universal spirit. It knows itself to be a divine spark from the great central sun of spirit. This exalted state of illuminated self-awareness has been variously termed 'spiritual consciousness,' 'Christ consciousness' or 'I AM consciousness.'

This dual-stage realization of the higher spiritual self has been concisely described, together with accompanying developmental initiatory exercises, by Yogi Ramacharaka in *Raja Yoga or Mental Development* (2007) as follows:

> The Yogi Masters teach that there are two degrees of this awakening consciousness of the Real Self. The first, which they call "the Consciousness of the I," is the full consciousness of *real* existence that comes to the Candidate [for initiation], and which causes him to *know* that he is a real entity having a life not depending on the body—*real* life, in fact. The second degree, which they call "the Consciousness of the I AM," is the consciousness of one's identity with the Universal Life, and his relationship to, and "in-touchness" with all life, expressed and unexpressed. These two degrees of consciousness come in time to all who seek "The Path." To some it comes suddenly, to others it dawns gradually; to many it comes assisted by the exercises and practical work of "Raja Yoga."

Following the attainment of spiritual consciousness, the ontological argument, 'I am, therefore God exists,' becomes not only an a priori truth held in the mind; but even more importantly, a first-hand spiritual experience grounded in reality. Syllogistically, the experience of 'I AM consciousness' can be expressed as follows:

1. The true ego (I AM) is spirit and exists in reality
2. The individualized spirit is one with universal spirit
3. Therefore, universal spirit (God) exists in reality

# CHAPTER 5

# THE COSMOLOGICAL ARGUMENT FOR GOD'S EXISTENCE

## 5.1 The Basic Argument and the Beginning of the Universe

CURRENTLY, the cosmological argument for God's existence has become a much more credible and persuasive proof due primarily to the findings of twentieth-century cosmology and astrophysics. Modern scientific research now confirms the traditional religious belief that the universe had a beginning. If the universe had a beginning, then it logically had a cause, according to the following syllogism:

1. Everything that begins to exist must have a cause
2. The universe began to exist
3. Therefore, the universe had a cause

Scientific understanding cannot explain at this time what caused the cosmic singularity to expand; in the unadorned words of cosmologist, Alan Guth (b.1947), the "instant of creation remains unexplained." Theologians, of course, affirm that the cause of creation was the supraphysical, spiritual activity (will) of God.

When 'Big Bang ripples,' background cosmic microwave radiation, were first observed in 1965 (by Arno Penzias and Robert Wilson of Bell Telephone laboratories) and later confirmed in 1992 (from the NASA Cosmic Background Explorer satellite), science historian and theologian Frederick B. Burnham remarked, "These findings, now available, make the idea that God created the universe a more respectable hypothesis today than at any time in the last 100 years."

Prior to Big Bang theory, most scientists believed that the universe was self-existent, without a beginning or end. Moreover, since the Big Bang singularity is calculated to exist outside the laws of the known universe, beyond the dimensions of physical space-time in a condition of potentiality, the idea of a supernatural cause for the universe now appears to be a much more reasonably sound conclusion. Expert scientists readily admit that the actual birth of the physical universe is beyond the epistemic grasp of natural science. Nobel Prize winning physicist, Leon M. Lederman (b.1922), expressed this curious state of affairs in *The God Particle: If the Universe is the Answer, What is the Question?* (1993):

> In the very beginning, there was a void, a curious form of vacuum, a nothingness containing no space, no time, no matter, no light, no sound. Yet the laws of nature were in place and this curious vacuum held potential. A story logically begins at the beginning, but this story is about the universe and unfortunately there is no data for the very beginning—none, zero. We don't know anything about the universe until it reaches the mature age of a billion of a trillionth of a second. That is, some very short time after creation in the big bang. When you read or hear anything [scientific] about the birth of the universe, someone is making it up—we are in the realm of philosophy. Only

God knows what happened at the very beginning.

The cosmological argument for God's existence, also known as the "argument from universal causation," the "argument from first cause" and the "causal argument," has been around for a very long time. Plato in *The Laws* (Book X) introduced the concept of a "self-originated motion" to account for the movement and activity of the cosmos. Aristotle in his *Metaphysics* postulated a first cause, a "prime mover" or "unmoved mover" that organized and set into motion the underlying substance of the universe. Aristotle's argument was later adapted by Thomas Aquinas in *Summa Theologica*, where he asserted that the universe must have been caused by something that was itself uncaused ("ex motu") which, as a Christian theologian, he concluded was a personal God.

Post Big Bang theory, the most familiar contemporary philosophical version to extend Aquinas' line of reasoning is the kalam cosmological argument introduced by American philosopher and theologian, William Lane Craig (b.1949). With the kalam argument, once the premise of a universal beginning is established from Big Bang theory, as well as the a priori necessity of a universal cause (as shown above), then the logical reasoning proceeds according to the following classical syllogism:

4. The chain of cause and effects cannot go back to infinity (that is, infinite regression is an impossibility)
5. Therefore, there must be a first cause to the universe
6. The first cause is God

As far as relying on the Big Bang singularity, though the preceding line of reasoning has merit in establishing a first cause (a cause that is itself uncaused) for the universe, the nature of that cause remains scientifically undefined: it could be something inherent in the cosmic singularity itself that caused it to expand or some external, impersonal, unknown supernatural agency that caused it to expand. The argument still doesn't conclusively establish a personal God as the first cause.

## 5.2   Logical Problems with the Cosmological Argument

While Big Bang theory has certainly given new life to the classical cosmological argument for God's existence, contemporary versions are not without unique logical difficulties. For instance, since the cosmic singularity existed before the creation of space and time, the usual cause and effect relationships don't necessarily apply: if there is no time, how can there be a cause that existed temporally 'before'? This dilemma can be addressed by positing the existence of 'metaphysical time.' Austrian philosopher and esotericist, Rudolf Steiner (1861–1925), in fact, claimed that prior to the beginning of time there existed a non-temporal, spiritual condition of "duration":

> [O]ur evolution for the first time passes over from a purely spiritual, inner existence into one manifesting externally … What is called "time" first makes its appearance, for the preceding states are not at all temporal. They belong to the region that in spiritual science may be termed "duration." (*An Outline of Occult Science*, 2011)

Using the beginning of the universe as the Big Bang singularity also produces a fault of equivocation in the first and second premises of the cosmological argument. Equivocation occurs when the same word being used in an argument has different meanings; in this case, it is the verb, 'to begin.' In the first premise, "Everything that begins to exist" refers to everything beginning in time; in the second premise, "The universe began to exist" refers to a beginning before time. Unfortunately, this fault in logic does weaken the argument somewhat.

A further objection to the cosmological argument is the question commonly raised of "What caused the first cause"; or conversely, "Why is the first cause unique and exempt from having a cause?" In other words, if God is equated with the first cause, what caused God to exist? As British evolutionary biologist Richard Dawkins (b.1941) has stated in *The God Delusion* (2008), Thomas Aquinas' cosmological argument makes "the entirely unwarranted assumption that God [the first cause] is immune to regress."

Though common, this particular objection is rather surprising and puzzling since it misses the entire point of the cosmological argument, which is to logically demonstrate the necessity of an uncaused cause that does not regress to infinity. Moreover, prior to the formulation of a Big Bang beginning, empirical scientists were quite content to regard the universe as infinite, eternal, self-existent and *uncaused*. Surely the notion of a self-existent, non-regressable creator is not that scientifically unreasonable or improbable to consider. Similarly stated prior to Big Bang theory by American theologian, Milton Valentine (1825–1906), in *Natural Theology* (1885):

> To substitute a self-existence of the universe, with its incalculable multiplicity of parts and interdependences, and countless human personalities, for the self-existence of God, multiplies the mystery a thousand-fold. The self-existence of God, therefore, offers less difficulty than the self-existence of the world. It is a reduction of the mystery to its lowest terms, to absolute unity and simplicity. It is therefore scientific, and challenges acceptance by its being the most reasonable [according to Occam's razor, the "law of parsimony"].

## 5.3 The Mystical Version of the Cosmological Argument

As with the ontological argument, there is a deeper, more mystical version of the cosmological argument for God's existence as well. With the initiatory experience of I AM consciousness, the true ego mystically experiences itself as a limitless, eternal and self-existent centre of consciousness and reality. The spiritual I experiences itself existing beyond mutable time in the eternal "Now" and beyond finite space in the infinite "Here." Similarly expressed in the form of spiritual advice in *Divine Healing of Mind and Body* (2004) by Murdo MacDonald-Bayne:

> Your true nature is Divine, let this nature become yours now, because now is Eternity, every moment of life is NOW. Therefore remember not the past nor be anxious for the future; the future is taken care of, by your living now. You must all come to the understanding of the Omnipresence that fills all space, knows nothing of past or future but is eternally present, the same yesterday, today and forever ... You still observe distances, days and months, times and years. This is the illusion of time and space. See yourselves in the Kingdom of Heaven; the same spirit within you is the same that created the world. When you understand this, you will see beyond the world of time and space ... If you overcome the sense of time and space, you shall also enter into this understanding where all is NOW, where there is no separation, no distance, no time.

Applying the mystical knowledge of spiritual consciousness to the cosmological argument in the form of a logical syllogism:

1. The true ego (I AM) is self-existent, uncaused spirit
2. The individualized spirit is one with universal spirit
3. Therefore, universal spirit (God) is self-existent and uncaused

# CHAPTER 6

# THE TELEOLOGICAL ARGUMENT FOR GOD'S EXISTENCE

## 6.1 The Basic Argument

IN RECENT DECADES, the teleological argument for the existence of God has also become the renewed subject of widespread and intense philosophical debate among scientists, theologians and philosophers. As with the cosmological argument, this heated discourse has been rekindled and refuelled by scientific discoveries in theoretical physics as well as detailed research in the life sciences such as biochemistry, genetics and evolutionary biology.

The teleological argument, otherwise known as the "argument from design," basically argues that if nature or the universe displays evidence of purpose, direction, design or intentional order then there must be an underlying intelligent designer (God) involved. Syllogistically, the basic version of this argument can be expressed as follows:

1. Purposeful order and complexity (design) requires an intelligent designer

2.  The universe (or some aspect of it) displays evidence of design
3.  Therefore, the universe has an intelligent designer (God)

This argument, like the cosmological and ontological arguments, has a long and august history extending back to the beginnings of the Intellectual Age. Plato, in the *Republic*, for example, postulated an underlying order and intelligence to the universe and in *Timaeus* he termed the supernatural creative designer, the "Demiurge." Predictably, Aristotle also argued that the cosmos exhibited inherent purposiveness and direction, which he referred to in *Metaphysics* as the Prime Mover.

## 6.2   The Famous "Watchmaker Analogy"

Cicero, in *de Natura Deorum* (*On the Nature of the Gods*), was the first known philosopher to use what later became known as the "watchmaker analogy" in support of a teleological argument. The basic reasoning underlying this analogy is that if a stranger were to happen across an unfamiliar object, in this case a lost watch (sundial or water clock) whose overall shape and complex arrangement of parts were seen to fulfill a function or purpose (in this case the telling of time), then it would be logical to deduce that this object was deliberately fashioned by an intelligent designer. In Cicero's own words:

> When you see a sundial or water clock, you see that it tells time by design and not by chance. How then can you imagine that the universe as a whole is devoid of purpose and intelligence, when it embraces everything, including these artefacts themselves [human designs] and their artificers [human designers]?

As a follower of ancient Roman polytheism, Cicero's

teleological argument was not of course used to establish the existence of a monotheistic supreme being, but rather the existence of an undefined, divine intelligence throughout nature: "the divine power is to be found in a principle of reason that pervades the whole of nature." (Ibid)

The watchmaker analogy was later made famous by the English philosopher and theologian William Paley (1743–1805) in *Natural Theology* (1802) and was also widely used by thinkers such as scientist Robert Hooke (1635–1703), David Hume, Rene Descartes and Voltaire, who once remarked: "I'm puzzled by the world, I cannot deem the timepiece [the universe] real, its maker [God] but a dream."

Seventeenth century cosmology extended this popular analogy to the extent that the universe was even regarded as behaving like an enormous, mechanical cosmic clock operating in accordance with natural law that was set in motion by the divine horologist, God. In the words of philosopher-scientist, Robert Boyle (1627–1691):

[The universe] is like a rare clock, such as may be that at Strasbourg, where all things are so skilfully contrived, that the engine being once set a-moving, all things proceed according to the artificer's (God's) first design, and the motions ... do not require the particular interposing of the artificer, or any intelligent agent employed by him, but perform their functions upon particular occasions, by virtue of the general and primitive contrivance of the whole engine. (quoted in G. J. Whitrow; *Time in History*; 1988)

Muslim philosopher Ibn Rushd (Averroes), in the late twelfth century, teleologically argued that the combination of order and continual motion in the universe demonstrated intelligence, not accidence, and hence a supreme principle of pure intelligence. Thomas Aquinas, who was thoroughly familiar with Averroist translations, postulated a famous teleological argument as one of his five proofs for God's existence. In *Summa Theologica* he stated:

> The fifth way is taken from the governance of the world. We see that things which lack knowledge, such as natural bodies, act for an end, and this is evident from their acting always, or nearly always, in the same way, so as to obtain the best result. Hence it is plain that they achieve their end, not fortuitously, but designedly. Now whatever lacks knowledge cannot move towards an end, unless it be directed by some being endowed with knowledge and intelligence; as the arrow is directed by the archer. Therefore, some intelligent being exists by whom all natural things are directed to their end; and this being we call God.

## 6.3  Purposeful Design versus Complexity

Present day critics of the teleological argument point out that complexity in Nature does not necessarily indicate arrangement by design, evidenced by computer programs (such as Weasel, Avida and Biomorphs) that can produce highly complex systems from a series of small, randomly-generated steps. This criticism, however, completely misses the point of the watchmaker analogy. It is not that the found watch exhibits complexity, but that it exhibits *purposeful* complexity; the complex arrangement of the individual parts is designed to perform a function, in this case, to tell time.

Similarly, with complex biological systems, the teleological argument is that they demonstrate purposeful arrangement, not just complexity. The human eye, for example, is more than just a complex arrangement of molecules; the eye performs a function—it enables the human subject to see.

Interestingly, even teleological critics such as Richard Dawkins are forced to admit that biological systems clearly appear to be designed:

> Living objects ... look designed, they look overwhelmingly as though they're designed. But it's terribly, terribly tempting to use the word designed ... But I've told you that they are not designed and coined the special word 'designoid.' (Royal Institute Christmas Lecture 2: *Designed and designoid objects*; 1991)

Dawkins reinforces this observational admission in *The God Delusion*:

> One of the greatest challenges to the human intellect, over the centuries, has been to explain how the complex, improbable appearance of design in the universe arises. The natural temptation is to attribute the appearance of design to actual design itself. In the case of a man-made artefact such as a watch, the designer really was an intelligent engineer. It is tempting to apply the same logic to the eye or a wing, a spider or a person.

Supporters of biological evolution maintain that living complexity has not been designed but instead results from the twin, non-intelligent mechanisms of chance variation and natural selection. In the case of natural selection, the insensate mechanical forces of nature act as a 'blind designer' using cumulative trial-and-error to 'select' and 'choose' chance adaptations (mutations) that are advantageous for survival (that is, for organisms to live and reproduce). Innumerable, random increments of organic change that are naturally selected over vast aeons of time are seen by evolutionists to account for the design-like complexity of living things and hence do not require any intelligent designer, divine or otherwise.

## 6.4   The Fatal Flaw of Logic in Evolutionary Theory

While observable change in the appearance and characteristics (phenotypes) of organisms over time, progressing from simple to more complex biological forms, is clearly evidenced and recognized, the argument of modern evolutionary theory for unintelligent, undesigned organic change has one, obvious fatal flaw. Natural selection is purported to have no purpose in mind, yet selection is determined to advance the survivability of a living organism and organisms exhibit a will to survive. As Dawkins has stated, "propagating DNA ... is every living object's sole reason for living." (Christmas Lecture Guide; *Growing up in the universe*; 1991)

A direction for natural selection and an organism's reason for living are clearly evolutionary purposes, and in accordance with the first premise of the teleological argument: "Purposeful order and complexity requires an intelligent designer"; where there is purpose, there must be intelligence behind it. Expressed syllogistically:

1. All physical arrangements that have a purpose have been created by an intelligent designer
2. According to evolutionary theory, living organisms are physical arrangements whose purpose is to survive and to replicate
3. Therefore, living organisms have been created by an intelligent designer

The remarkable conclusion, then, of modern evolutionary theory is that rather than being a refutation of the teleological argument, it instead provides logical support for the idea of an intelligent designer—even the idea of God. And even though the evolutionary idea that living organisms possess a will to survive and propagate readily admits that there is a purpose to life—what a crude, simplistic and unimaginative purpose!

It is difficult to comprehend how serious scientific thinkers can actually admit to supporting such a horrid reductionism. Do they actually believe that the single, entire meaning of human life is simply to propagate DNA? As remarked earlier, no human being, including theory of evolution supporters, could possibly lead their lives according to such a crude notion. They couldn't possibly get out of bed in the morning, go to work, or get an education, or publish a paper, or lecture on TV, or attend a conference or music concert with this one basic urge as their sole motivation—to spread their DNA. If it were so, then their credentials would simply be their sperm count and the number of children produced, not PhDs or Nobel prizes, and they certainly wouldn't waste valuable reproductive energy arguing that God doesn't exist.

## 6.5   The Statistical Improbability of Accidental Design

Evolutionary theory, as an explanation for the beginning of life, has also been on the run since the scientific discovery that the universe had a beginning only a scant 13.7 billion years ago. It was much easier to argue that the astounding complexity of living organisms was the result of a lengthy string of chance chemical accidents when the length of time needed could be stretched back to infinity. This propitious condition, unfortunately for evolutionists, was no longer mathematically available with the reality of a young, finite universe.

Severely limiting the time for biological complexity to evolve has, of course, astronomically increased the statistical improbability that living systems were developed accidentally and not by design. Moreover, the more that biological science understands living organisms and the processes of life, the more purposefully complex they continue to become.

Research chemist Robert Shapiro (b.1935), for example, has calculated that the probability of even a basic organism such as a bacterium spontaneously emerging with the proper order of amino acids is an astonishing 1 in $10^{100,000,000,000}$. Given such odds, this is clearly impossible.

Astronomers Fred Hoyle and Chandra Wickramsinghe have calculated the probability that life could originate from non-life as 1 in $10^{40,000}$. Hoyle more picturesquely described the unlikely odds of life originating on earth by chance as similar to the odds that a hurricane sweeping through a junkyard could perfectly assemble a Boeing 747. Physicist Hubert P. Yockey (b.1916), who founded the field of information theories that apply to molecular biology, has calculated that in order for life to arise by natural processes, the age of the earth needs to be in excess of 10 to the one hundred billionth power years old. To place these unfathomable numbers in some perspective:

1. The age of the universe is $10^{18}$ seconds old
2. The number of stars in the universe is $10^{22}$
3. The number of atoms in the universe is $10^{80}$

While numbers can certainly be used for and against any argument and though probability statistics regarding life widely vary, few (if any) informed present-day thinkers would deny that, mathematically speaking, it is extremely improbable that life has occurred by chance. Even staunch evolutionist, Richard Dawkins, commenting on laboratory, origin-of-life experiments admits: "it is still possible to maintain that the probability of its happening [from chance inorganic chemistry] is, and always was, exceedingly low—although it did happen once." (*The God Delusion*)

## 6.6    The Multiverse Theory versus the God Hypothesis

In what is clearly a desperate attempt to negate the enormous improbability calculations resulting from a young, finite universe—a universe with limited time and resources—macroevolution supporters have advanced the purely hypothetical notion of infinite universes ( a "multiverse") instead. Not only is there no evidential support for this idea, but the equations of general relativity guarantee that we can never discover another universe since the space-time manifold of one universe can never overlap the space-time manifold of another (that is, there would be no contact between universes). Moreover, logically considered, the appeal to infinite universes commits an "inflationary fallacy" by multiplying probabilistic resources without independent evidence.

At the present time, then, it would appear that there are two, main, competing explanations for the appearance of design and complexity in living organisms: (1) the hypothesis of intelligent design (God), and (2) the multiverse evolutionary theory. Concerning these competing concepts, astrophysicist Guillermo Gonzalez (b.1963) has stated:

> World Ensemble [multiverse] advocates are obviously driven by the desire to avoid the "God-hypothesis" … in adopting such extravagant and unnecessary assumptions. (with Hugh Ross; *Home Alone in the Universe*; 2000)

## 6.7 The Incredible Fine-tuning Necessary for Organic Life

Scientific research from numerous disciplines has increasingly combined to evidence that physical life, as we know it, is entirely dependent on numerous, extremely specific universal and terrestrial constraints. Even the slightest variation in any one of these necessities prevents physical life from occurring. Life chemistry, for example, requires the assembly of complex molecules.

Unless electromagnetic force has a specific value, molecules will not assemble. If electromagnetism is too weak, the electron will not orbit the nucleus. If electrons can't orbit, they can't be shared with other nuclei and hence no molecules. If electromagnetism is too strong, electrons can't separate from the nucleus to be shared, and once again no molecules. If the nuclear force is too strong, protons and neutrons will forcibly attach to other protons and neutrons thereby preventing the formation of hydrogen. Without hydrogen, there is no familiar organic chemistry. If the nuclear force is only slightly weaker, then protons can't attach to neutrons resulting in the sole formation of hydrogen throughout the universe. Life chemistry requires more than just hydrogen.

Also, if the neutron were slightly less massive than it is now, the universe would create too many neutrons and quickly collapse into neutron stars and black holes, thereby making life impossible. If the neutron were slightly more massive, there wouldn't be enough of these particles created to make carbon, oxygen, nitrogen and the other elements that are essential for life.

In order for planets, stars and galaxies to form, gravity must be the dominant force in the universe. But since gravity is $10^{40}$ times weaker than electromagnetism, the universe must be electrically neutral to enable gravitational prominence. The number of protons must be almost equal to the number of electrons to cancel each other out. Slightly too many of either particle (anything more than 1 out of $10^{37}$) would upset that cosmic neutrality and prevent life. The total mass of the universe is also critical for life to exist. If the mass density of the universe is too great, nuclear fusion is enhanced resulting in the conversion of all hydrogen into elements heavier than iron. Once again, no carbon, oxygen, nitrogen—no organic life. If the universe has too little mass, then nuclear fusion is inefficient producing nothing but hydrogen and a bit of helium.

If the universe is too old or too young, then conditions aren't favourable for life chemistry either. Life is only possible around late-born stars that have the heavy elements necessary for life—and only spiral galaxies produce the requisite stars. Of the trillion estimated galaxies in the universe, only 6% are spiral galaxies. Even within a likely spiral galaxy, life is not possible too close to the centre where the intense gravity would destroy planetary orbits; or too far from the centre where there are insufficient heavy elements from exploding supernovae remnants to enable life chemistry.

One essential life element, fluorine, unfortunately is not formed by supernovae explosions but only on the surfaces of white dwarf binaries. It looks as though any galaxy that has the right number of special white dwarf binaries in the right place and at the right time for life to exist is extremely rare; in fact, our own Milky Way galaxy may be the only one.

Not surprisingly, life is also dependent on proximity to a sun of a specific size. If the sun is too big, it burns too rapidly and erratically to maintain a long-term, stable heat source to make life possible. If the sun is too small, it doesn't burn as hot thereby requiring any life-sustaining planet to be positioned closer in order to maintain the correct temperature. An aqueous planet that is too close to a sun cannot establish the required rotational period due to disruption of the tidal forces. If planetary rotation is too fast or too slow, life cannot exist. If rotation is too fast, there are too many hurricanes and tornadoes produced. If the planet rotates too slowly, the temperature is too hot during the day and too cold at night to sustain life.

The life-sustaining planet also needs to be a specific size. If the planet is too massive, it retains too much ammonia, methane, hydrogen and helium to be conducive for advanced living organisms. But if the planet isn't massive enough, it can't retain enough water to support life.

While the many foregoing examples of specific life requirements are only a miniscule and simplified sampling, it is nonetheless obvious from modern scientific research that physical life can only occur within exceedingly narrow cosmic parameters. Scientific literature and scientific commentary popularly refer to these critical physical constants and constraints as "fine-tuning," prompting some theorists to conclude that the existing universe is purposefully fine tuned to permit life, particularly human life. The anthropocentric observation that human beings occupy a special position in a universe that is favourable designed for life has been loosely termed the "anthropic principle."

While the term, anthropic principle, was first coined in 1973 by theoretical astrophysicist, Brandon Carter (b.1942), and later popularized by cosmologist, John D. Barrow (b.1952) and mathematical physicist, Frank J. Tipler (b.1947) in *The Anthropic Cosmological Principle* (1986), the idea itself has been around for much longer. In 1904, for instance, evolutionary biologist Alfred Russel Wallace (1823–1913) stated:

> Such a vast and complex universe as that which we know exists around us, may have been absolutely required … in order to produce a world that should be precisely adapted in every detail for the orderly development of life culminating in man. (*Man's Place in the Universe*)

Due to its many variations and interpretations, the anthropic principle has become a rather confusing concept and consequently has been used to both support and refute the teleological argument from intelligent design. The observable fact that human beings exist in a life-friendly environment is not surprising since it doesn't make sense to occupy an environment where life is impossible. What is surprising from the numerous, narrow, physical limitations is that such a life-friendly environment exists at all, given the overwhelming mathematical improbability of such an environment existing.

While planet earth obviously provides conditions amenable to carbon-based life forms, no other planet in our vast universe of a trillion galaxies has been found that duplicates or even approximates earthly conditions. While the universe may be fine tuned to make life possible, it clearly isn't fine tuned to enable a profusion of earth-style life forms to exist throughout the cosmos. Nevertheless, advocates of the teleological argument regard the improbability of chance chemical biogenesis and the observations of cosmic fine-tuning as strong evidence of an intelligent designer. In the words of British cosmologist, Edward Harrison (1919–2007):

> The fine-tuning of the universe provides prima facie evidence for theistic design. Take your choice, blind chance that requires an infinite number of universes, or design that requires only one.

## 6.8   Objections to Intelligent Design

Unfortunately, but not unpredictably, the logical argument for intelligent design has become negatively associated with the politically active, intelligent design movement in the United States. The ID movement has been funded and supported by the Discovery Institute, a conservative think-tank that promotes religious activism such as the suppression of evolutionary theory and the inclusion of creationism[9] in public school science classes (which currently contravenes the constitutional separation of church and state). Of course not all proponents of the argument from design are supporters of the intelligent design movement, the Discovery Institute or creationism.

Teleologically speaking, intelligent design can be a

perfectly valid, rational inference from scientific data and not a deduction from religious authority. The notion of intelligent design, unlike creationism, is not based on biblical references. Nevertheless, arguments from intelligent design can certainly be used to provide religious support or used to promote social and political agendas. It is faulty logic, however, the "psychogenetic fallacy," to dismiss an argument such as intelligent design on the basis of the religious beliefs of its supporters or on the basis of an organization to which these supporters belong.

A common, though illogical, objection to the teleological idea of a cosmic intelligent designer is the question of "Who designed the designer?" It is not at all necessary to answer this question to reasonably conclude that a purposeful complexity has a designer. For example, it is not necessary to know the heredity of Egyptian stonemasons to conclude that the pyramids had a designer. Moreover, the question invites an infinite regress that is logically unacceptable. As explained by William Lane Craig:

> It is widely recognized that in order for an explanation to be the best explanation, one needn't have an explanation of the explanation (indeed, such a requirement would generate an infinite regress, so that everything becomes inexplicable ... believing that the design hypothesis is the best explanation ... doesn't depend upon our ability to explain the designer.

A similar objection also completely misses the point of the argument from design: "If the complexity of living organisms is highly improbable, then a divine designer would be even more complex and even more improbable." The improbability in this case, however, is not that life exists but the improbability that life exists as the result of blind chance and blind selection, hence the need to invoke an intelligent designer as a logical solution. A very high improbability of chance means a high probability of design which increases, not decreases, the likelihood of an intelligent designer—whatever the designer's nature. To use a previously mentioned analogy, the improbability that a 747 jumbo jet was constructed by a hurricane in a junkyard does not mean that Boeing engineers are more complicated and hence more improbable; the improbability of blind chance logically increases the strong possibility of intelligent design. Besides, no religious thinker logically conceives that God, the cosmic designer, could ever be created by chance.

## 6.9   Nanobiology, DNA and Intelligent Design

The teleological argument from design has been given enormous weight and persuasiveness from increased knowledge since the 1950s of the sub-cellular world of nanobiology. The term, "simple cell," has quickly become an oxymoron. Microscopic cellular structures and mechanisms are now recognized to be astonishingly complex, specialized and self-directive—being commonly referred to as "nanotechnology" and "biomolecular nanomachines." The propulsive units of certain bacteria flagella (the long, thin, tail-like locomotive structures) look remarkably like miniature rotary motors, complete with distinct mechanical parts composed of proteins: rotors, stators, O-rings, bushings, U-joints and drive shafts (See Figure 1 below).

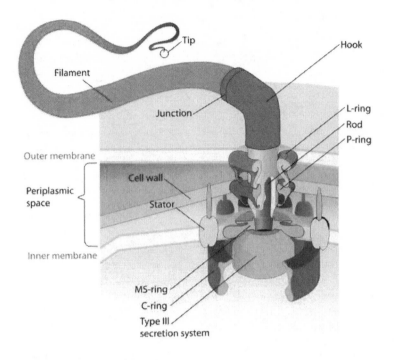

**Figure 1**: Diagram of Bacteria Flagellum

To even a casual observer, the appearance of design is undeniable. As stated by biophysics researcher, Keiichi Namba, "An enormous number of those macromolecules play each role just like purposefully designed machines and maintain the complex network activities."

Even the basic molecular building blocks of the cell—proteins—are complex, twisting three-dimensional chains of at least twenty carefully sequenced amino acids. Yeast proteins average 466 amino acids long and the largest protein, connectin (important in the contraction of striated muscle tissue), consists of 34,350 amino acids. The formation of complex and functionally specific cellular proteins does not occur by chance; but rather, protein biosynthesis is directed by an even more complex molecule within the cell, deoxyribonucleic acid—DNA.

The remarkable property of the DNA macromolecule is that it is able to store and transmit information necessary for protein production in the exquisitely precise, multiple sequencing of four nucleotide bases: adenine, thymine, guanine and cytosine that are specifically arranged along the spine of the molecule's helical strands (see Figure 2 below). These nucleotide bases (represented with the letters A, T, G, and C) function in precisely the same way as symbols in a machine code (such as in a computer), hence the term "genetic code" (see Figure 3 below). In the words of Richard Dawkins, "The machine code of genes [a segment of DNA] is uncannily computer-like." Echoed by Microsoft founder, Bill Gates, "DNA is like a computer program. But far, far more advanced than any software we've ever created."

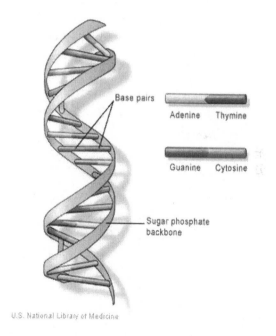

**Figure 2**: DNA Molecule showing nucleotide bases

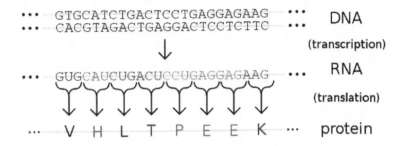

**Figure 4:** DNA Genetic Code Sequencing

Certain proponents of the teleological argument from design maintain that a code is clearly the product of intelligence since the fundamental property of any code or language is that it symbolically represents something other than itself in order to convey information. For example, when archaeologists stumble across some unknown markings that appear to convey information in a symbolic form, they reasonably infer intelligent configuration. In efforts to search for extraterrestrial intelligence (SETI), any aperiodic radio signals from space that exhibit "specified complexity" or "information content" would be regarded as an indication of intelligent life. Expressing this variation of the teleological argument syllogistically:

1. All codes and languages are designed by intelligence
2. DNA is a genetic code
3. Therefore, DNA has been designed by intelligence

Critics have objected that this line of reasoning commits the fallacy of equivocation since they allege that the word "code" has two different meanings: (1) "code" as a human invention and (2) "code" as a formation of nature. Supporters define a code by its performance, not by its source, asserting that the reason scientists refer to DNA as a code is not poetic, like the pancreatic "islands of Langehans," but because it clearly acts as a code—encoding, decoding, storing and transmitting information. The DNA genetic code is also regarded as equivalent to a written language and not just analogous. As stated by Hubert Yockey: "It is important to understand that we are not reasoning by analogy. The sequence hypothesis [of the genetic code] applies directly to the protein and the genetic text as well as to written language and therefore the treatment is mathematically identical." ("Self Organization Origin of Life Scenarios and Information Theory"; 1981)

The smallest known, free-living organism, the microbe Nanoarchaeum equitans, has a genome (the total DNA sequence that characterizes a species) composed of 490,885 base pairs (nucleotide bases that are conjoined: adenine with thymine, guanine with cytosine). In comparison, the human genome is an organized complexity of 3.2 billion nucleotide pairs. Interestingly, the Amoeba dubia has the largest genome discovered to date, over 200 times larger than the human genome, an astounding 670 billion base pairs.

The statistical impossibility of complex proteins being produced by chance has been scientifically explained by the directive, chemically programmed activity of DNA. But in the case of DNA, how did it occur? Where is the selective mechanism in nature that overcame the impossible odds of chance formation to assemble this complicated biogenetic molecule? As with protein synthesis, the chance formation of DNA is statistically impossible:

> The probability of making DNA of any simple organism by chance with all ingredients available is 1/10 with 60 million zeros. The probability of picking out one specific grain of sand from the sea is estimated as 1/10 with 15 zeros. Even a billion chemical reactions a second over billions of years would only provide 1/10 with 158 zero chances ... It is safe to say then that by any means of trial and error the chances of making functioning DNA by time and chance are unequivocally impossible. (K. Dean

Reeves. Internet article, "DNA Not by Chance")

While the statistical impossibility of complete cellular DNA being assembled by chance is widely accepted, it has been argued that since natural selection is a cumulative process, when the end product is divided into a lengthy series of smaller, highly improbable occurrences that are combined over a long period of time, then the impossible becomes possible. Unfortunately, such logic is analogous to arguing about the possibility of winning a thousand lotteries in a row. Just because it's possible (though highly unlikely) of winning a single, million-to-one lottery doesn't mean that it's now statistically possible to cumulatively win the next nine hundred and ninety-nine lotteries in a row. Besides, the argument still does not address the question of what natural agent or mechanism was doing the selection to establish the original, self-replicating molecular ancestor of DNA. Nor do macro-evolutionary proponents address the more philosophical question: "Why would lifeless atoms want to assemble themselves into a supermolecule in order to replicate and perpetuate a complex 'life-form' in the first place?"

Staunch supporters of evolution admit to the current inadequacy of the theory in explaining the origin of life, but defend it nonetheless as the best possible explanation developed thus far. Postulating a divine designer is regarded as an appeal to ignorance that fills in a clear gap in scientific knowledge with the actions of a hypothetical God (pejoratively termed "the God of the gaps"). It is felt that just because there is no physical mechanism to explain biogenesis at the present time does not mean that one will not be discovered sometime in the future. It is also objected that proponents of intelligent design are equally unable to alternatively explain in reasonable detail how physical life was divinely designed.

Despite being used for conservative American social,

political and religious agendas, the centuries-old teleological argument from design has been a persuasive and reasonable proof of God's existence for many serious contemporary thinkers. British philosopher and prominent atheist, Antony Flew (b.1923), for example, captured worldwide attention when he announced in 2004 that he was now convinced of the existence of a deistic first cause, an "Aristotelian God who has the characteristics of power and also intelligence." In a published interview that year, Flew stated:

> I think that the most impressive arguments for God's existence are those that are supported by recent scientific discoveries. I've never been much impressed by the kalam cosmological argument, and I don't think it has gotten any stronger recently. However, I think the argument to Intelligent Design is enormously stronger than it was when I first met it ... It now seems to me that the findings of more than fifty years of DNA research have provided materials for a new and enormously powerful argument to design. (*Atheist Becomes Theist—An Exclusive Interview with Former Atheist Antony Flew*, 2004)

From what has been here indicated by Flew, it is expressly ironic that the most powerful and convincing support for the teleological argument for God's existence has come, not from theology or philosophy, but from the recent discoveries of natural science.

# CHAPTER 7

# THE RATIONAL ARGUMENT FOR GOD'S EXISTENCE

## 7.1 The Basic Argument

OTHERWISE KNOWN as the "argument from reason" and the "argument from mind," the rational argument for God's existence is not as familiar as the preceding three philosophical proofs, though it has enjoyed a recent surge of interest and debate. It is often subsumed within the ontological argument as an "argument from consciousness" or within the teleological argument as an "argument from intelligence."

While the existence of a conscious mind certainly has strong ontological connections with an individual's essential being (in fact, it's impossible to envision true personhood without a conscious mind) and clearly it also has teleological connections since intelligent design requires an inventive, purposeful mind, the distinct argument from reason has uniquely-compelling philosophical features of its own.

In its most basic conceptual form, the argument from

reason is a kind of transcendental or presuppositional argument that can be syllogistically expressed as follows:

1. If reason exists, then God exists
2. Reason exists
3. Therefore, God exists

Similar to the basic ontological argument, this unadorned version of the argument from reason relies entirely on internal a priori logic excluding any need for evidential support. In this form, the argument suffers from the weakness of circular reasoning: it assumes from the beginning what it intends to establish by its conclusion—the existence of God. There are, however, more persuasive versions of the argument.

## 7.2  A Brief History of the Argument from Reason

The general notion that the existence of human minds presupposes an originating universal mind of course extends back to the time of Plato. The more specific idea that the process of thinking itself can be used as an argument in favour of theism, as opposed to materialism or determinism, originated primarily with Immanuel Kant, as evidenced in the second edition of *Critique of Pure Reason* (1998):

> From this [argument] follows the impossibility of any explanation in materialist terms of the constitution of the self as a merely thinking subject.

British Prime Minister Arthur Balfour later developed the argument from reason in *The Foundations of Belief* (1905) as logical grounds for accepting theism as opposed to "naturalism";[10] as did philosopher James Bissett Pratt (1875–1944) in *Matter and Spirit: A Study of Mind and Body in Their Relation to the Spiritual Life* (1922) and Oxford philosopher H.W.B. Joseph (1867–1943) in *Some Problems With Ethics* (1931). In the 1940s, this line of reasoning was popularized and refined by British novelist and essayist C.S. Lewis (1898–1963). Lewis provided a concise summary of his argument, which he termed "The Cardinal Difficulty of Naturalism," in the essay "Is Theology Poetry?" (1944):

> If minds are wholly dependent on brains, and brains on biochemistry, and biochemistry (in the long run) on the meaningless flux of the atoms, I cannot understand how the thought of those minds should have any more significance than the sound of the wind in the trees.

One example of how Lewis extended this line of reasoning as an argument for the existence of God was given in *The Case for Christianity* (1996):

> Supposing there was no intelligence behind the universe, no creative mind. In that case, nobody designed my brain for the purpose of thinking. It is merely that when the atoms inside my skull happen, for physical or chemical reasons, to arrange themselves in a certain way, this gives me, as a by-product, the sensation I call thought. But, if so, how can I trust my own thinking to be true? It's like upsetting a milk jug and hoping that the way it splashes itself will give me a map of London. But if I can't trust my own thinking, of course I can't trust the arguments leading to Atheism, and therefore have no reason to be an Atheist, or anything else. Unless I believe in God, I cannot believe in thought: so I can never use thought to disbelieve in God.

More recent philosophers such as Victor Reppert (b.1954) in *C.S. Lewis' Dangerous Idea* (2003), William Hasker (b.1935) in *The Emergent Self* (1999) and Alvin Plantinga in *Warrant and Proper Function* (1993) have acknowledged and expanded Lewis' argument. Individual variations of the argument from reason have also been defended by philosopher and theologian J.P. Moreland (b.1948) in *Scaling the Secular City: A Defense of Christianity* (1987) and philosopher Richard Swinburne in *Evidence For God* (1986).

While there are numerous subtle variations of the argument from reason being advanced today, not all presenters are theistic advocates, some are simply critics of the current naturalist explanation of the human mind. And even though some presenters do not support the notion of a mind-body dualism, most advocates of the argument postulate the existence of an immaterial mind that is distinct from the physical brain (body).

## 7.3 The Immaterial Nature of the Human Mind

Even though as human beings we directly experience the non-physical, immaterial nature of the mind, it is clear that most individuals are consciously unaware of, and therefore underappreciate, the importance and unique characteristics of our internal mental processes and items. The four basic and distinct mental processes of thinking, feeling, willing and perceiving have very different features from physical processes—and the corresponding mental items of thoughts, emotions, intentions and perceptions likewise do not share the essential characteristics of physical items.

Physical items, for instance, possess spatial extension: they have length, width and height. When referring to a mental item such as a thought or feeling, however, it is inapplicable to consider how tall or how wide it is. Physical items are also quantifiable, they can be weighed and measured; but once again, it is incongruous to determine the heaviness or measurable amount of a mental item, such as a pound of thought or a cup of feeling (though poetically a thought might "weigh heavy upon the heart").

Physical events and items, according to natural science, happen and occur as the result of fixed chemical law; they simply are what they are and nothing more. In the mind, however, physical processes are transformed and qualitatively experienced. In the mind, the physical action of air vibrating 440 times a second is not perceived simply as rapidly moving air; but is qualitatively experienced as a musical "A" note. Likewise, even more rapidly vibrating electromagnetic radiation is not experienced as simply chemically-induced movement; but rather subjectively experienced as the colour green or blue. Moreover, in the physical world a rock is only a rock; whereas in the mental world, a rock can be a symbol for strength, or the name of a forceful man ("Peter" is 'rock' in Latin) or a metaphor for Christ (the "Rock of Ages").

Mental processes and items are also invisible to empirical observation. Individual thoughts, feelings, willful intentions and sensations are entirely private and internal, accessible exclusively to the subject who experiences them. No external observer, scientist or otherwise, can physically perceive the interior mental landscape of another. The chemical and neurological activity of the brain can certainly be physically explored and studied, but subjective mental experiencing of physical brain activity remains empirically inviolable and sacrosanct.

From the foregoing examples, it is clear that the inner workings of the mind do not conform to the deterministic chemical processes of the physical universe. Furthermore, the fact that human minds can establish purpose, direction and meaning in an otherwise purposeless, directionless and meaningless universe also contravenes the very foundational assumptions of the physical universe according to the natural scientific worldview. Moreover, consciousness and intelligence also light up in human minds out of a universe that is scientifically claimed to be non-intelligent, insensate and blindly mechanistic. Expressing these objections syllogistically:

1. Naturalistic physical causes are fundamentally non-rational, non-purposeful and non-aware
2. The human mind is capable of expressing conscious rationality and purpose
3. Therefore, the human mind cannot be the result of naturalistic physical causes

## 7.4   The Logical Flaws of a Material Mind

Proponents of the argument from reason (or mind) characteristically find natural scientific explanations of the mind inadequate and untenable. American neurophilosopher Paul Churchland (b.1942) has concisely expressed the general naturalist position:

> The important point about the standard evolutionary story is that the human species and all of its features are the wholly physical outcome of a purely physical process ... If this is the correct account of our origins, then there seems neither need, nor room, to fit any non-physical substances or properties [such as minds and mental phenomena] into out theoretical account of ourselves. We are creatures of matter. And we should learn to live with that fact. (*Matter and Consciousness*; 1984)

In order to pinpoint the faulty reasoning with such typical, pro-naturalism statements, it can be syllogistically outlined as follows:

1. If we are merely the result of naturalistic evolutionary processes, then we are wholly physical creatures
2. We are merely the result of naturalistic evolutionary processes
3. Therefore, we are wholly physical creatures

In this form, it is now apparent that such an argument commits the fallacy of circular reasoning, thereby begging the question by assuming the very thing it is attempting to deduce—that we are wholly physical creatures (premise 2 would not be accepted as true unless conclusion 3 is already accepted). Proponents of the argument from reason do not of course accept premise 2, and restate the argument as follows:

4. If we are merely the result of naturalistic evolutionary processes, then we are wholly physical beings
5. We possess non-physical conscious minds, so we are not wholly physical beings
6. Therefore, we are not merely the result of naturalistic evolutionary processes[11]

## 7.5 The Mind-Brain Duality

It is quite understandable that naturalistic philosophers and natural scientists have difficulty accepting or even considering the notion of a non-physical, immaterial mind. From everyday experience and ordinary sensory observation, there is no mind without a brain. There decidedly appears to be a mind-brain dependence; mental activity does not appear to occur without some form of material, computational substrate (in this case, a brain). A number of observations can be cited as evidence for mind-brain dependence. For instance, the phylogenic evolution of the brain correspondingly develops increased cognitive capacity. Individual ontogenic brain development also enables and enhances mental ability. Conversely, brain damage from accidents, toxins, diseases and malnutrition often result in permanent loss of mental functioning. The chemical effects of various drugs such as alcohol and LSD have a corresponding effect on mental activity. Electrical stimulation of the brain can invoke memories, perceptions and desires, indicating a connection between brain states and mental states. Formulated as an argument from physical mind, this evidence has been effectively used to argue the case for atheism.

While the dualistic separation of mind and brain may seem foreign and contrary to many contemporary natural scientists, the notion of an independently existing mind distinct from the body can be traced back to the writings of Plato and Aristotle, as well as to the Sankhya and Yoga schools of Hindu philosophy (c.650 BC). By distinguishing a non-extended, non-physical mind from the somatic brain, Rene Descartes was the first dualist thinker to formulate the problem of mind-body interaction that is familiar today, particularly within the branch of philosophy known as the "philosophy of mind." The independent existence of a supraphysical mind, which manifests through the physical vehicle of the body, has also been a foundational principle of the esoteric tradition of the East and West for hundreds of years.

Since ancient times, philosophers have proposed that the brain acts as an intermediary between mind and body. Hippocrates (c.460 BC – 377 BC), for example, described the brain as "the interpreter of consciousness." While acknowledging that there is clearly a strong and intimate mind-brain connection (a functional dependence between the brain and the mind), it is not necessarily a 'productive function' in the sense that the brain 'produces' consciousness and mentation, that mental states are an effect of chemical brain states. The brain can and should also be considered as having a 'permissive function' (analogous to turning on a light switch) and a 'transmissive function' (analogous to a prism permitting light to pass through it). The switch does not produce the light but electrically permits it; and neither does the prism produce the light but simply transmits it. This argument was summarized by William James in his Ingersoll Lecture in 1898:

> My thesis now is this, that, when we think of the law that thought is a function of the brain, we are not required to think of productive function only; we are entitled also to consider permissive or transmissive function. And this, the ordinary psychophysiologist leaves out of account.

When the brain is regarded more as a bodily organ of reception and transmission for the self-existent mind, then the observational evidence for a strictly material explanation for the mind can be, instead, explained dualistically. In the case of a radio receiver, for example, though a musical broadcast is certainly dependent on the physical apparatus of the radio, the sound is ultimately produced by invisible electromagnetic radio waves, not by the apparatus itself. Positively or negatively altering components of the physical receiving equipment will certainly affect the sound, but not the original radio signal. Similarly with mind-brain interaction, invisible non-physical mental activity will induce chemical, electrical activity in the physical brain. Positively or negatively altering the physical apparatus of the brain will certainly affect its receptive ability (and hence the behaviour of the human subject), but this does not extinguish the independent thought signals of the mind.

Not only do mental states affect brain states, but brain states will also affect mental states. The brain, then, also functions as a somatic transmitter as well as a receiver, conveying sensory information to the mind. Altering the physical apparatus of the brain will also affect the activity of the mind: the thoughts, feelings, actions and perceptions that occur. In the case of, say severe brain damage, the mind may be deprived of important, stimulating sensory information. Though severely restricted in its interaction with the physical world, thereby limiting the experiences of the human subject, the non-corporeal mind will still continue to function in a decreased capacity.

The postulation that mind and matter, thought and brain cell, are fundamentally distinct kinds of substances is philosophically termed "substance dualism" or "Cartesian dualism" (after Descartes who famously defended this idea). Substance dualism, not surprisingly from the very beginning, has been shadowed by what has often been called "the problem of interactionism": how can an immaterial mind interact with a material body, and vice versa. While many thinkers have regarded psychosomatic interaction as an insurmountable hurdle, it is easily overcome by referring to the similar interaction of matter and energy. Energy, being imperceptible and immaterial, is fundamentally distinct from matter, yet it impinges on matter and causes it to move (or to do work). Likewise, the immaterial 'mental energy' of the mind intelligently stimulates and directs neurochemical activity by impinging on the grey matter of the brain. Empirically, as with energy, we observe the invisible immaterial agent (in this case, mind) only indirectly through the induced changes in physical matter (in this case, brain states).

## 7.6  Mind-Brain Interaction According to Spiritual Science

It can be objected that the matter-energy analogy does not apply in this instance since matter and energy are not fundamentally different substances, but rather two states of the same substance (since they are interconvertible according to Einsteinian relativity). While agreeing with the substantive relationship of matter and energy, esotericists and spiritual scientists would counter that energy is itself a condensed or lower vibratory form of 'mind stuff' or mental energy;

therefore mind, energy and matter can all be regarded as various states of the same substance. This relationship also helps explain why mind and matter can interact.

When observed clairvoyantly in spiritual scientific investigation, mind-body interaction is seen to be a complicated process. A thought does not impinge directly onto the physical material of the brain, but requires a number of necessary intermediary processes. Once a thought has congealed in the mind (in 'mind stuff'), it must surround itself with astral or soul material ('desire stuff') since there must be a 'driving impulse' connected to the idea in order to proceed further. The emotively charged thought then presses upon the life energy field ('etheric force') that permeates and vitalizes all organic material, and this sets in motion the observable physical chemistry in the brain.

Mirroring the incredible complexity of physical organic chemistry, the supraphysical processes involved between mind and body are equally detailed and specific. It is not surprising, then, that even strong proponents of dualism have difficulty answering the problem of interactionism, particularly without supersensible observation. Nevertheless, detailing this interaction is not necessary to conclude that mental states are non-material and therefore inexplicable by naturalistic means.

Directly experiencing the supersensible nature of the mind is also one of the primary goals of spiritual scientific training (initiation). While the very idea will certainly be outlandish to the dedicated materialist, naturalist or physicalist, the cultivation of brain-free thinking is a necessary component for authentic spiritual perception. As detailed by Rudolf Steiner in *An Outline of Esoteric Science* (1997):

> [Initiatory meditative exercises] serve to free the human soul from sensory perception and from the brain, the instrument to which our intellect is initially bound ... The first thing we experience on this path is the process of

being freed from our physical organs. We can say that our consciousness is not extinguished when we disregard sensory perceptions and ordinary intellectual thinking; we are able to rise above them and experience ourselves as individual beings alongside what we were previously. This is the first purely spiritual experience—observing an "I"-being of soul and spirit, a new self that has risen up out of the self that is bound only to the physical senses and the physical intellect [of the brain].

## 7.7    Universal Mind and Universal Being (God)

Defenders of naturalism consistently maintain that the fundamental physics of the universe is non-rational, lifeless and purposeless. Since they are forced to acknowledge that human beings are rational, alive and purposeful, some have explained this glaring contradiction by arguing that mind, consciousness and the characteristics of life are essentially physical features that emerge once a sufficient level of molecular complexity is obtained. This argument is the foundational thesis of "emergent materialism" and "property dualism." Unfortunately, the idea that intellection, awareness and vitality just somehow 'emerged' from matter is a weak argument since emergence is simply a label for the phenomena being explained, rather than an actual explanation of how something appears to come from nothing.

The argument from reason or mind clearly has philosophical merit in arguing the inadequacy of naturalistic explanations of mind and consciousness. It is still rather tenuous as an argument for God, however, though a case can certainly be made. For example, if individual minds are indeed non-physical and have a common origin, then it is reasonable to conclude that they are the products of a universal mind. Since minds are always associated with persons (or beings), a universal mind would likely be the possession of a universal being; that is, God. Syllogistically, this argument can be outlined as follows:

1. Individual human minds always belong to individual human beings
2. A universal mind must belong to a universal being (God)
3. Therefore, God exists

# CHAPTER 8

# THE MORAL ARGUMENT FOR GOD'S EXISTENCE

## 8.1 What is Morality?

BEFORE EXAMINING the moral argument for God's existence, it is first necessary to clarify what morality means. Morality, to many, is an ambiguous term that can generally be defined as an ideological system concerning right and wrong conduct. More specifically, morality can be understood in three distinct, fundamentally different ways.

Firstly, there is what may be termed "practical, relative or subjective" morality: a particular code of conduct established by society, philosophy, religion or personal conscience that is held to be authoritative in matters of right and wrong. Morality in this sense is "descriptive"; that is, it describes real-life moral behaviour that has actually occurred.

Secondly, the term morality is also used in a more all-inclusive universal sense to refer to an ideal code of conduct that is supposedly shared by all rational people under similarly specific conditions. Morality in this sense is a "perfect, absolute and objective" code of conduct that has not been completely identified or entirely realized, but rather exists in the mind ideally. Since objective morality is regarded as an ultimate standard of conduct for all, it is characterized as "normative"; and since this usage of morality refers to how rational people *should* or *ought* to behave rather than simply describing ways that they *do* behave, it is also characterized as "prescriptive." Objective or prescriptive morality, then, can be viewed as the innate moral potential of all rational people to do the universally right thing; whereas subjective, descriptive morality refers to the actual dynamic practice of doing the right thing (disregarding considerations of what *should be* the right thing).

Thirdly, the term morality is often used synonymously with ethics, a major branch of philosophy that includes the study of right and wrong conduct. The philosophy of ethics, however, is much broader than the exclusive study of moral conduct and also includes the central consideration of "the good life": ideas of what constitutes a life worth living and issues around obtaining satisfaction in life. Further clarified, morality is antecedent to ethics: it denotes the prior fact of rightful conduct of which ethics is the philosophical study.

The philosophy of ethics examines moral conduct from five main sub-disciplinary viewpoints:

1. "Descriptive ethics": is the value-free, observational study of the moral choices that people make and abide by in actual practice.
2. "Normative ethics": is the study of how moral values should be determined, of what makes actions right and wrong.
3. "Applied ethics": is the study of how a moral outcome can be achieved in a specific situation, of how to apply ethical theory to real-life situations.
4. "Meta-ethics": is the study of the fundamental nature of morality and whether it has any objective justification.

5. "Moral psychology": is the study of how moral capacity develops and the nature of that capacity.

The philosophical study of ethics was established several centuries prior to the first formulation of the moral argument for God's existence. Socrates, for instance, correlated knowledge with virtue and virtue with happiness. The truly wise person, according to Socrates, will do what is right and good and will thereby achieve happiness. For Aristotle, self-realization was the key to virtue and happiness. A person acting entirely in accordance with their true nature and realizing their full potential will do what is right and good, thereby obtaining true happiness.

## 8.2   The Kantian Postulation on Morality and God

Of the philosophical arguments for God's existence that have been examined thus far, the moral argument is the most recent, having been formally proposed for the first time (more as a postulation than a proof) by Immanuel Kant in *Critique of Pure Reason*. Since then the moral argument has taken numerous forms, all of which attempt to demonstrate the existence of God from the observation of morality in the world. No doubt the timing of Kant's familiar moral argument (postulation) was stimulated by the burgeoning claim of eighteenth-century naturalistic science that the world was governed by morally blind causes. How then do moral considerations arise from amoral forces? This question continues to fuel modern regard for the moral argument.

In its most general form, which varies from Kant's version, the argument can be syllogistically expressed as follows:

1. Human beings direct their behaviour according to purposeful moral considerations

2. Purposeful moral activity cannot arise from purposeless, morally-blind physical causes

3. Therefore, morality is the result of supraphysical causation; that is, God

Kant began his variation of the argument with a similar initial premise, that moral behaviour is fundamentally rational: we have good reason to be moral. This good reason is dependent on there being justice to moral behaviour: unrighteous behaviour has painful negative consequences; righteous behaviour has pleasurable positive consequences. If there were no unpleasant just-consequences for immorality, then there would be no reason to be moral. Since justice is not always administered in a single lifetime, since people don't always 'get what they deserve,' since life often appears unfair, since immoral people can profit from crime and since bad things happen to good people, there must be divine justice administered after death—hence the existence of God.

According to Kant, moral virtue lawfully leads to true happiness, the "summum bonum" ('highest good') of human existence. Human beings are therefore rationally impelled to seek the summum bonum of life. Kant's basic argument may be syllogistically simplified as follows:

1. Moral behaviour is rational; there is good reason to be moral

2. There is rationality, good reason, for moral behaviour only when there are fair and just consequences incurred

3. Fair consequences may need to be spiritually apportioned after death for justice to be ultimately done (so there must be an eternal God)

Though Kant's philosophical reasoning most strongly argued for the necessity of some spiritual process of after-death justice in order for morality to reasonably exist, this conclusion need not be exclusively theistic; for example, there may be some impersonal mechanism of post-mortem justice involved. Since God has traditionally been regarded as the source of posthumous justice, however, it was not unreasonable or surprising for Kant to postulate theistic existence in connection with his argument.

Moreover, Kant's theistic postulation was also bolstered by his contention that there exists a universal sense of moral obligation, which he termed the "categorical imperative." The existence of objective moral law, according to Kant, can only have its source in a supreme being, God. As stated in *Critique of Pure Reason*:

> It is our duty to promote the highest good; and it is not merely our privilege but a necessity connected with our duty as requisite to presuppose the possibility of this highest good. This presupposition is made only under the condition of the existence of God, and this condition inseparably connects this supposition with duty. Therefore it is morally necessary to assume the existence of God.

## 8.3   God as the Absolute Standard of Morality

The existence of universal, objective moral law; that is, moral absolutes such as absolute goodness, is of course much easier to accept if one already accepts the existence of an absolute God. God, in this case, becomes the absolute standard of goodness. Goodness, then, can be regarded as the degree of 'god-ness' that an individual embodies; the more one behaves like God, the more one is morally good.

Together with the existence of an absolute standard for moral conduct (God, in this case), actual moral practice and application will understandably vary according to time, place, age, person and circumstance. Objectively-based moral principles, then, can also be relatively applied according to any number of physical and psychological conditions. The existence of moral principles need not be an exclusive choice between absolute moral values or relative moral values—they both can equally co-exist. If one only subscribes to a relative material universe, however, a universe devoid of any absolute spiritual ground of reality, then human behaviour, in consequence with all physical activity, will logically be regarded as strictly relative. It is therefore much more difficult for the naturalist thinker to embrace objective moral law than it is for the religious thinker to acknowledge moral relativity (though moral relativity may be rejected as inferior).

Nevertheless, natural scientists do postulate the existence of universal physical laws (the law of gravity, for instance) that operate relative to specific conditions (such as mass, distance, time and velocity). Universal objective moral law is resisted, of course, because it requires intelligence, purpose, and being which are naturalistically excluded from the recognized materials and forces of the physical universe. From a naturalist perspective, then, Kant's moral argument is often rejected on the basis that there is nothing observed in moral conduct that exclusively demands a divine lawgiver as the source. Yet natural science is unable to adequately explain how and why complex msolecular configurations (human beings) conform their behaviour, not aimlessly according to chemical law, but to purposeful impulses of right and wrong, goodness and badness. Where do these moral impulses come from, since they cannot logically arise from morally blind and aimless mechanical forces?

## 8.4 Euthyphro's Dilemma

Critics of the Kantian argument from morality have also rejected this line of reasoning on the basis of a perceived contradiction in God being postulated as the ultimate standard of moral law—the divine lawgiver. This particular objection (in its various guises) centres around the question: "Is an action good because God commanded it, or did God command it because it is good?" This philosophical perplexity was not first raised in connection with Kant's moral argument, but has been intellectually pondered at least since the time of Plato, becoming subsequently known as "Euthyphro's Dilemma," since that was the name of the Platonic character who first voiced the dilemma. The basic problem is whether or not morality can be established simply on the basis of authority. If 'good' were solely determined by a command of God, then any action such as murder or rape would be deemed 'good' if God commanded it. This horn of the dilemma is obviously morally unacceptable. On the other horn, if God is compelled to issue good commands according to some objective basis, this implies the existence of a transcendental morality, apart from God, that would inviolate God as the absolute standard of morality.

While critics of the Kantian moral argument have concluded from the Euthyphro dilemma that the postulation of God being the moral standard is logically fallacious, proponents of the argument maintain that the dilemma can easily be resolved—which was previously done so by St. Thomas Aquinas. Aquinas had already argued that the moral commands of God are indeed good, not from authority and not from some external moral reference, but because God always acts in accordance with his inner nature which is essentially good.

## 8.5   C.S. Lewis' Argument from Morality

Another well-known theistic argument from morality was propounded by C.S. Lewis in *Mere Christianity* (2009). Lewis began his argument with the premise that there exists an absolute, objective moral law. He then assumed that these objective moral laws are very peculiar and quite unlike laws of nature and natural facts. For instance, objective moral law cannot be animalistic herd instinct since moral law often acts contrary to personal and group survival. Objective moral law cannot be mere convention either, since it may also act contrary to existing social values. As well, objective moral law cannot be a physical law of nature since it is prescriptive ('what ought to be') rather than descriptive ('what actually is'). Since objective moral law is an 'ought' rather than an 'is,' it must reside in a mind, instead of in matter. The source of objective moral law cannot be part of the material universe but must reside in an absolutely good transcendent mind (that is, God). Syllogistically formulated, Lewis' argument may appear as follows:

1. There exists an absolute, objective moral law
2. Absolute, objective moral law, being unlike the laws of nature, has its source in a transcendent mind (a divine moral lawgiver)
3. That transcendent mind (divine moral lawgiver) is God

Many critics have refuted Lewis' argument by challenging the existence of an absolute, objective moral law. Interestingly, while not accepting moral absolutes, many critical thinkers have recognized the necessity of some form of moral universalism, some shared or agreed upon standard of moral conduct. If all morality is entirely subjective personal choice, if everyone established their own subjective morality and adopted their own personal standards of right and wrong, then there would be no basis for denouncing the behaviour of others as wrong if that behaviour was acceptable by the personal standards of the other. Hitler, for example, could not be denounced for committing genocide if he was acting in accordance with his own acceptable moral standards. In the words of American linguist, philosopher and cognitive scientist, Noam Chomsky (b.1928):

> [I]f we adopt the principle of universality: if an action is
> right (or wrong) for others, it is right (or wrong) for us.
> Those who do not rise to the minimal level of applying to
> themselves the standards they apply to others—more
> stringent ones in fact—plainly cannot be taken seriously
> when they speak of appropriateness of response; or of
> right and wrong, good and evil. ("Terror and Just
> Response"; 2002)

One commonly suggested universal moral standard is:
"Right action is whatever produces the greatest good (or
happiness) for the greatest number of people." Without some
absolute moral grounding, however, the question immediately
arises: "Why should we be concerned about the welfare of
others?"

A second logical objection to Lewis' argument from
morality states that even if the first premise of an absolute,
objective moral law is accepted, the source isn't necessarily
God but perhaps, as Aristotle suggested, our common human
nature. Also, even if the second premise of a transcendent
mental source is accepted, moral absolutes could result from
the existence of platonic archetypal ideas, for example, rather
than from God. While these objections are valid,
understanding how moral absolutes spring from a non-
spiritual human nature or from discarnate mental forms may
prove more difficult than the God-hypothesis.

## 8.6   Evolutionary Theory and Morality

Evolutionary theory, of course, attempts to explain the
observations of moral conduct from a non-theistic
perspective. Since, according to evolution, the activity of all
living organisms is directed entirely and exclusively to

surviving and reproducing, what is observationally described as moral conduct in human beings is simply behaviour that has evolved through chance and natural selection over millions of years that contributes to continued survival. What is 'right' advances survivability and what is 'wrong' impedes survivability. Expressions of empathy, altruism and self-sacrifice are simply behaviours directed to the survivability of the species, which indirectly perpetuates the individual's DNA through kinship (familial) survival. Some scientific theorists, such as Vittorio Gallese (b.1959), have even associated human empathy with hypothetical "mirror neurons"[12] in the brain; the implication being that empathy is not a compassionate moral choice, but an involuntary, electrochemical cerebral firing.

Morality, as conceived by evolutionary theory, is a reductionist distortion of any worthy notion of selflessly compassionate morality since it is ultimately self-centred and selfish—being exclusively concerned with self-preservation. This conclusion can be clearly illustrated by a series of prescriptive moral questions and answers:

Q: According to evolutionary theory, the prime directive for all individual organisms is to survive and reproduce. So, why should each individual not act selfishly?

A: Because it is harmful to the social group (family, community, country).

Q: So, why should individuals be concerned with the health of the social group?

A: Because if social groups don't survive, then the species doesn't survive.

Q: So, why should individuals care about the species?

A: Because if the species dies out, then the individual will not survive.

Q: So, why then should individuals act unselfishly?

A: Because it's better for the individual.

According to the dictates of evolutionary theory, then, individuals should 'morally' act unselfishly in order to further their own selfish interest.

A moral code based on selfishness is certainly not morality as commonly defined or understood. In fact, such a morality is diametrically opposed to overall Christian morality which de-emphasizes the separate personal ego associated with the physical biological self and encourages the compassionate, spiritual self in unity with Christ. The following examples reflect this unselfish Christian morality:

> Then Jesus told his disciples, "If any man would come after me, let him deny himself and take up his cross and follow me. For whoever would save his life will lose it, and whoever loses his life for my sake will find it. For what will it profit a man, if he gains the whole world and forfeits his [spiritual] life? (Matt 16: 24–26; RSVCE)

> You have heard that it was said, "You shall love your neighbour and hate your enemy," But I say to you, Love your enemies and pray for those who persecute you, so that you may be sons of your Father who is in heaven." (Matt 5: 43–45; RSVCE)

> For I through the law died to the law, that I might live to God. I have been crucified with Christ; it is no longer I who live, but Christ who lives in me; and the life I now live in the flesh I live by faith in the Son of God, who loved me and gave himself for me. (Gal 2: 19–20; RSVCE)

It is also difficult to comprehend from an evolutionary perspective why complex chemical configurations (human beings, for example) are concerned about how they *ought* or *should* behave. Does vinegar worry about how it ought to behave towards baking soda? Besides, morality implies conscious, rational choice between right and wrong. If living organisms are determined entirely by blind, mechanical physical forces, shouldn't human behaviour be equally mechanically blind and predictable, and move in exactly the same non-rational, purposeless manner as one billiard ball when struck by another? If the billiard ball isn't concerned with the moral choice of "turning the other cheek" or "seeking revenge" after being senselessly hit, why are chemical man-machines so concerned?

The existence of human morality is clearly another area of human experience that exposes the everyday duplicity of strong evolution-theory defenders: they live their lives by a universal moral code entirely contrary to the selfish morality prescribed and restricted by their naturalist worldview. Evolution champion, Richard Dawkins, at least demonstrated honesty and insight when he publicly admitted to this behavioural dichotomy: "I'm a passionate Darwinian when it comes to science, when it comes to explaining the world; but I'm a passionate anti-Darwinian when it comes to morality and politics" (*The Science Show*, ABC Radio; 2000).

## 8.7 Morality Requires Existence of God not Belief in God

The theistic argument from morality, by definition, connects the existence of morality with the existence of God. Critics will often misinterpret the argument to mean that *belief* in God is a precondition of morality, whereas what is actually being argued is that the *existence* of God is the necessary precondition of morality. Belief in God does not necessarily equate with virtuous moral behaviour: atheists may be strong moral practitioners while TV preachers may have pronounced moral failures. It reasonably follows that if there does exist a personal God of absolute goodness, then that goodness would be instilled in all created beings whether they acknowledged their Creator or not. Hence, a virtuous atheist is no evidence that morality can exist without God; but rather, demonstration that the universal reality of God is not dependent on the vicissitudes of each human mind.

The notion of divinely instilled or innate spiritual goodness common to all human beings has been philosophically debated for many years. French philosophers Jean-Jacques Rousseau (1712–1778) and Pierre-Simon Ballanche (1776–1847) supported the notion of an innate moral sense, while English philosophers John Locke (1632–1704) and John Stuart Mill (1806–1873) denied any such inherent principle and considered conscience to be simply a faculty of moral discrimination acquired through experience.

A variation of the moral argument, using the idea of a divinely-instilled moral conscience as the fundamental premise, was also propounded by John Henry (Cardinal) Newman (1801–1890). As he himself stated:

> When he became Creator, he implanted this law, which is himself, in the intelligence of all rational creatures. The divine law, then, is the rule of ethical truth, the standard of right and wrong, a sovereign, irresistible, absolute authority … This law, as appreciated in the minds of individual men, is called 'conscience.' ("Letter to the Duke of Norfolk"; 1874)

The common possession of an intrinsic, God-given moral conscience does not, of course, imply that all individuals are compelled to abide by that intuitive moral sense. Some may choose to disregard and thereby weaken their moral conscience, while others may choose to follow and thereby strengthen their moral conscience. Conscience, then, is not necessarily static, unchanging or perfectly realized; but a potential capacity for good that develops towards moral perfection the more it is exercised and applied.

## 8.8   The Rational Problem of Evil

No examination of morality or any theistic moral argument would be complete without some consideration of the problem of evil. It has been historically difficult for theists and non-theists alike to reconcile the observation of terrible evil in the world with the conception of an omnibenevolent (perfectly good), omniscient (all-knowing) and omnipotent (all-powerful) creator God. The Greek philosopher Epicurus (c.341 BC – 270 BC) is generally credited with being the first thinker to delineate the rational problem of evil, since known as the "Epicurean paradox" or the "riddle of Epicurus," articulated as follows:

> Either God wants to abolish evil, and cannot; or he can, but does not want to. If he wants to, but cannot, he is impotent. If he can, but does not want to, he is wicked. If God can abolish evil, and God really wants to do it, why is there evil in the world? (Epicurus, according to Lactantius in *The Wrath of God*)

Not surprisingly, the problem of evil has often been used as a philosophical argument against the existence of God. While the atheistic argument from evil is actually a family of arguments, this family often appears in four principal attires:

1. "The argument from unbelief": the existence of agnostics and atheists (the capacity of God-denial) is proof that God does not exist.
2. "The argument from imperfection": the existence of an imperfect world is proof that a perfect Creator does not exist.
3. "The argument from natural evil": the existence of natural disasters such as floods, hurricanes, earthquakes, forest fires, tsunamis, tornadoes, volcanic eruptions and devastating storms is proof that a loving, benevolent God does not exist.

4. "The argument from moral evil": the existence of pain, suffering, torture and death that is wilfully inflicted upon the world by free moral agents (human beings) is proof that God does not exist.

Despite the familial peculiarities and complexities, the atheistic argument from evil can be syllogistically generalized into the following form, known as the "inconsistent triad":

1. If God were omniscient, omnipotent and perfectly good, then there would be no evil
2. There is evil in the world
3. Therefore, God does not exist

The entire atheistic family of arguments from evil can also be sorted into two distinct camps on the basis of the primary logical reasoning utilized in the argument. One class of argument relies mainly on a priori, deductive logic (also known as the "logical problem of evil"); the other class relies more on a posteriori, inductive logic (also known as the "evidential problem of evil").

The deductive arguments claim that there is a logical contradiction in asserting the existence of God together with evil; that it is logically impossible that both God and evil exist, analogous to postulating a square circle. The main proponent of this line of reasoning in more recent years was Australian philosopher, J.L. Mackie (1917–1981).

The evidential arguments do not assert that the existence of God and the fact of evil are logically incompatible, but rather that the observational range and depth of seemingly gratuitous, pointless evil is strong evidence against an all-powerful, all-loving God. The objection in this case is not that theism is logically inconsistent, but that it is implausible: it lacks a reasonable explanation for the existence of meaningless evil. One modern-day proponent of this line of reasoning was American philosopher, Wesley C. Salmon (1925–2001), who used a statistical approach to argue that a mechanical model of the universe was probabilistically better at explaining the existence of evil than was the improbable premise of an all-wise, benevolent creator God.

## 8.9 Refuting the Argument from Evil: Defenses and Theodices

The theistic response to the various arguments from evil has been in two primary ways: a "defense" or a "theodicy." A defense attempts to refute a specific argument from evil by demonstrating that the existence of God and observable evil are not inconsistent or improbable. A theodicy, on the other hand, attempts to provide a true and reasonable explanation of why God allows evil to exist. Contemporary theists have been more interested in providing defenses rather than theodices.

One very effective defense in rebutting Mackie's logical argument has been provided by Alvin Plantinga (b.1932) and is known as the "free-will defense." The backbone of Plantinga's defense (as with all similar defenses) rests on challenging some incorrect assumptions often made concerning omnipotence and omnibenevolence. Being all-powerful does not mean that God can do anything. For instance, God cannot create a logical contradiction or a logical impossibility such as a square circle, a married bachelor or a rock too large for him to lift. Also, God cannot act in contradiction to his character; he cannot be something he is not. Omnipotence, then, is redefined to mean that God has no non-logical limits to what he can do.

Concerning omnibenevolence, this does not mean that a perfectly good being such as God will always eliminate evil. It can be reasonably argued that a good being can allow evil and still remain good if there is a good reason to allow it. Omnibenevolence, then, is redefined to mean that God always eliminates evil unless he has good reason to allow it.

So what possible good reason could God have to allow evil to exist? While it may be difficult to know with certainty the intentions of God, one possible good reason provided by Plantinga is the development and preservation of free-will, and thereby free moral choice. In order to create free moral beings with the capacity to willingly choose between good and evil, evil must exist as a possibility. Moreover, free moral beings must be able, by definition, to choose evil as well as good without external compulsion or constraint. To force one to do good or to prevent one from doing evil would violate true moral freedom. A free moral being forced to singularly choose good is a logical impossibility, a contradiction. God permits evil, then, for the greater good of creating free moral beings.

Plantinga's free-will defense is regarded by most contemporary philosophers to be a reasonable refutation to the deductive or logical problem of evil. As stated by philosopher and atheist, William L. Rowe (b.1931):

> Some philosophers have contended that the existence of evil is logically inconsistent with the existence of the theistic God. No one, I think, has succeeded in establishing such an extravagant claim. Indeed, granted incompatibilism, there is a fairly compelling argument for the view that the existence of evil is logically consistent with the existence of the theistic God. ("The Problem of Evil and Some Varieties of Atheism"; *APQ*; 1979)

The free-will defense, however, does not provide sufficient reason for all manner of evil in the world such as naturally occurring evils like hurricanes and earthquakes. It is difficult to attribute all such catastrophic evil with a misuse of free-will, though the large-scale disastrous effects of global climate change can be ascribed to the misuse of human technology and the earth's natural resources.

One possible theodicy for the human suffering caused by natural disasters is that humanity does not live in global isolation, but rather exists in intimate union with the entire planetary environment. What, from a human perspective, is a devastating lightning storm is, from a planetary perspective, a small, localized atmospheric electrical discharge that neutralizes the electrical imbalance in the air, thereby providing a more stable, life-sustaining habitat overall. Similar logic can be applied to earthquakes, hurricanes, tornadoes, and forest fires. It can also be argued that God has provided living creatures with adaptive evolutionary capacities such as intelligence, mobility, perception, sensation and instinct to minimize or avoid the harsh regional effects of powerful terrestrial forces and upheavals necessary to maintain the planetary equilibrium required for organic life.

A logical extension of the free-will defense can also be effectively and theodically used to answer the evidential problem of evil. This atheistic argument relies on the observed existence of gratuitous, unjustified evil in the world that supposedly negates the existence of a benevolent God. Once again, the argument fails if there exists possible good reason for God to allow extreme evil to occur.

A weak, though popular, theodicy is the possibility that God indeed has good reason, but since his wisdom and knowledge far transcends our own, we are unable to discern or comprehend what this good reason might be. Since it is not unreasonable to expect some mystery to the supernal intentions of God, the lack of human comprehension of evil cannot be used as evidence against his existence. This position characterizes what is known as "skeptical theism."

Plantinga has also provided a stronger theodicy for gratuitous evil by arguing that for free moral decisions to be significant and not trivial, the range of free choices available must also be significant and not restrictively narrow. For God to unduly limit the possibility of serious evil would seriously limit the range of free choice. Truly free moral beings must be capable of the highest good as well as the deepest depravity.

While Plantinga's reasoning certainly does deflect the evidential argument from evil, it also raises other interesting corollary questions; for example:

1. Does God continue to allow a significant range of moral choice after death?
2. Is there a 'day of judgement' where God separates those individuals who choose significant good from those who choose terrible evil?
3. Though it may be creatively necessary for God to not unduly restrict the free-will possibility of significant evil, isn't it morally responsible for humans themselves to prevent or confine others who commit serious and harmful evil, even though this restricts their free-will choices?
4. Is God anguished, sorrowed or heartbroken that some of his children persist in choosing the dark path of evil?

It is also worth mentioning that the problem of evil is a double-edged sword for non-theist thinkers, philosophically cutting both ways. By asserting the existence of absolute evil, it can be argued that the non-theist is unwittingly acknowledging an absolute standard of morality; that is, God. It can also be argued that by affirming the existence of evil, the non-theist is subscribing to a concept that was historically formulated by exclusively religious ideologies. If evil is more narrowly defined as a transgression against God, then it is illogical to argue that there is no God on the basis of the many horrific instances of transgressions (evil) against God. Moreover, it is difficult to understand why certain non-theists expect others to share their moral outrage with issues such as teaching creationism in public schools if, as they allege, there is no universal standard of morality. If right and wrong are simply arbitrary personal choices, the creationist position is just as morally right as their own, so why the indignation?

In conclusion, the long-term horrifying consequences of the practical denial of any absolute standard of morality; that is, God, has been chillingly described by the convicted serial killer, Jeffrey Dahmer (1960–1994):

> If a person doesn't think there is a God to be accountable to, then—then what's the point of trying to modify your behaviour to keep it within acceptable ranges? That's how I thought anyway. I always believed the theory of evolution as truth, that we all just came from the slime. When we, when we died, you know, that was it, there was nothing. (Dateline NBC; 1994)

# CHAPTER 9

# THE LOGICAL ATTRIBUTES OF THE ONE GOD

## 9.1   Using Logic to Also Understand the Nature of God

EVEN THOUGH MANKIND has suffered the experiential loss of the primal, innate connection with nature and the original sense of oneness with the supernatural world, the corresponding mental capacity of reason and logic that has been increasingly acquired throughout the Intellectual Age can instead be used to establish conceptual unity concerning the one reality that is God. Where once cosmic unity was unquestioned and instinctively felt, now in human development it must be sought for and intellectually conceived.

Through the sincere and assiduous application of intellectual thought, God "can be known with certainty through the powers of reason."[13] The intellect is not necessarily inimical to perceiving and understanding the Supreme Being. In fact, the challenge of extending our intellectual reach to the sublimity of God—back to the source of all creation—demands the highest, the clearest and the sharpest reasoning that the intellect is capable of. Poor conceptualization, imprecise logic and wooly-headed thinking will not scale the heights to the supernal summit.

Fortunately, the concentrated light of rigorous logic is a sure guide to truth in the celestial realms as well as the physical world. As emphasized by philosopher and esotericist Rudolf Steiner (1861–1925) in the lecture "The Stages of Rosicrucian Initiation" (1907):

> Those who truly know about the higher world understand that perceptions are totally different from perceptions in the physical world. One thing, however, does remain the same in the physical and astral [soul] worlds and in devachan [heaven], namely, logical thinking. This reliable guide protects us from all flighty and illusory thoughts. Without it, we never learn to distinguish illusion from reality and mistake every illusion for an astral [superphysical] reality.

Though God, as supreme being, logically extends far beyond the boundaries of the finite human mind, the application of logical thinking through techniques such as extrapolation, deduction, projection and analogy can cast the net of intellectual understanding far beyond its own limited shores. And while direct, first-hand spiritual experiencing is the most convincing proof of God's existence, a sound intellect can reliably lead us to the vast shoreline of the spiritual sea, from where we can catch a glimpse of the one reality that is God.

## 9.2   The Divine Nature is Infinite

Once intellectual certainty in the existence of the Supreme Being has been established, then a number of attributes belonging to the one nature logically flow from this realization. The clear light of logical reasoning can also be effectively and satisfyingly used to reveal transcendent truth about the spiritual nature of the one God.

For instance, if there is only one supreme reality, then that reality must be infinite, without internal or external restriction or boundary. If God had a boundary, then there would be something beyond or outside of God. Reality would not therefore be one, but two: God and 'something beyond.' Moreover, God would no longer be supreme if there was something greater that existed outside of the divine oneness. God must logically be everywhere in order to be the one and only reality.

While a condition of infinity, of absolute limitlessness, is a logical necessity of the one God, attempting to conceive or to visualize infinity can certainly be an exasperating exercise. Infinity is clearly outside the range of our ordinary, everyday experience which everywhere perceives finite forms and conditions—which perceives limitations to all things. Moreover, we often make the conceptual mistake of equating infinity with unlimited spatial extension. We try to visualize infinity by extending galactic space endlessly in all directions. But if physical space came into existence with the creation of the universe (according to the "singularity theorem"), then cosmic space is finite, limited and can't be stretched to infinity. Infinity existed prior to cosmic space, before the physical universe in all its immensity was created. Infinity, then, cannot simply be conceived as totally expanded space; it is infinitely beyond that.

Also, infinity cannot be properly comprehended by simply visualizing a condition without boundaries, margins, borders or edges. The two-dimensional surface of a sphere, for example, has no edge or boundary, yet it is finite and not infinite. Moving across a spherical surface will encounter no edge or boundary, but the surface is not infinite. Likewise, the universe itself may be without a cosmic margin or a physical boundary; yet it is finite and not infinite. The entire universe may have a two-dimensional, spherical-like topology due to the curvature of space-time predicted by Einstein's equations. Accordingly, a straight line projected uninterruptedly into cosmic space (such as a beam of light), will eventually return to the precise point of departure.

The curved nature of physical space as calculated by natural science is also supported by the esoteric research of Rudolf Steiner, as indicated by the following:

> The conception of space gave me the greatest inner difficulty [in 1880 at age nineteen]. As the illimitable, all-encompassing vacuity—the form in which it lay at the basis of the dominant theories of natural science—it could not be conceived in any definite manner. Through the more recent (synthetic) geometry, which I learned by means of lectures and in private study, there came to my mind the perception that a line which should be prolonged endlessly toward the right hand would return again from the left to its starting point. The infinitely distant point on the right is the same as the point infinitely distant on the left. It came over me that by means of such conceptions of the newer geometry one might form a conception of space, which otherwise remained fixed in vacuity. The straight line returning upon itself like a circle seemed to be a revelation. (*The Course of My Life*; 1970)

Also important to consider is the paradoxical nature of infinity. For one, infinity extends to the infinitely immense and to the infinitely minute at the same time. For another, since infinity is without limit in all directions, every location is logically the centre (the same is true on the surface of a sphere). In the words of twelfth-century theologian Alain de Lille (c.1128–1202) quoting from the third-century mystical text, the *Corpus Hermeticum*: "God is an intelligible sphere whose centre is everywhere and whose circumference is nowhere."

As a logical attribute of the nature of God, the necessity of being infinite had been philosophically deduced as far back as 600 BC. The Greek philosopher, Anaximander (c.610 BC–c.547 BC), conceived 'the boundless beginning' or "arche" ('first principle') as an endless, unlimited, primordial chaos that united the opposites of hot and cold, and wet and dry: the four fundamental conditions from which every manifested thing was believed to be derived. The "Isha Upanishad" of the Indian writing, *Yajurveda* (c.400 BC–300 BC), poetically conveyed the idea that God is infinite and that infinity could not be measured mathematically. The medieval philosopher John Duns Scotus (c.1266–1308) later conveyed the widely-held theological position that the term, "infinite," when applied to God meant "existing without constraint," rather than "being unlimited in quantity."

Furthermore, the infinite nature of God is logically more than simply being a condition without spatial constraint or confinement. If God is infinite, then all attributes of the one divine nature must also be characteristically infinite. God is, therefore, infinite in wisdom, love, mercy, joy, compassion and understanding. When extended to an infinite degree, all divine attributes of course become "perfections," the highest possible attainments. Succinctly stated as an infallible truth of the Catholic Faith: "God is actually infinite in every perfection."

The infinite attribute of God has also historically meant that the divine nature is regarded as being 'incomprehensible' to human beings. The archaic meaning of incomprehensible was "to have no limits; to be boundless." In this sense, then, incomprehensible does not mean that God's nature is utterly unknowable; but rather, that it is infinitely deep, well beyond the circumscription of any finite human mind. The infinite nature of God can certainly be partially and incompletely known, but total and perfect comprehension is logically beyond the intellectual reach of the finite human mind.

Nevertheless, according to St. Thomas Aquinas, intellectual attempts by the finite mind to meaningfully comprehend infinity are enabled and assisted by the immaterial nature of the mind. As stated in his *Summa Theologica*:

> The fact that the power of the intellect extends itself in a way to infinite things, is because the intellect is a form not in matter, but either wholly separated from matter, as is the Angelic substance or at least an intellectual power, which is not the act of any [physical] organ [such as the brain], in the intellectual soul joined to the body.

## 9.3   The Divine Nature is Eternal

As well as being infinite, the depth of intellectual logic also fathoms that the one God must be eternal, without temporal limitation or constraint. If the one reality is all that exists, then God must have always existed since there is nothing else inside or outside the divine nature from which to arise or to cause a beginning. Likewise, if there is nothing other than the divine nature into which it can change, transform or alternate then there can logically be no ending to God's existence. If God is the one and the all, then nothing existed before God and nothing can exist after God. God must have always existed and must continue to exist throughout eternity.

While theistic philosophers and theological thinkers logically agree that God is eternal, there is some disagreement as to the precise meaning of the word, "eternal." The traditional view from Augustine to Aquinas concerning the eternal nature has been that God is "timeless" or "atemporal," that the one reality exists outside or beyond the occurrence of time. According to this view, the eternal existence of the Supreme Being is not measured by an indefinite length of time or subject to any sequencing of time (such as past, present and future). Presently, however, the dominant view among modern-day philosophers is that God is "everlasting" and "temporal" in the sense that he exists forever in time. Both conceptions of eternity—timelessness and everlastingness—are still logically forced to maintain that the Supreme Being had no beginning and will have no end; that God has never come into existence and will never go out of existence.

The fact that there are differing philosophical conceptions of the eternal nature of God once again demonstrates the limitations of logical reasoning to definitively comprehend the Supreme Being. Not surprisingly, then, the defining of eternity as either timelessness or everlastingness is not a recent idea. For instance, the early medieval philosopher, Boethius (c.480–c.525), in *The Consolation of Philosophy* distinguished between timelessness which he attributed to God, and everlastingness which characterized the world according to platonic philosophy:

> [F]or it is one thing to progress like the world in Plato's theory through everlasting life, and another thing to have embraced the whole of everlasting life in one simultaneous present [as in God].

Central to any understanding of God's eternal timelessness is Boethius' notion of "one simultaneous present," the idea that God does not experience events in chronological succession according to past, present and future; but all at once in the eternal Now. This fundamental conception was also understood by Augustine who wrote in *Confessions* (397–398):

> [I]n eternity nothing passes but all is present, whereas time cannot be present all at once ... Who shall lay hold upon the mind of man, that it may stand and see that time with

its past and future must be determined by eternity, which stands and does not pass, which has in itself no past or future.

Augustine also provided a helpful analogy to comprehend God's timeless existence. Human memory, he suggested, is similar to God's interaction with the temporal world in that a whole series of prior sequential events can be called to mind simultaneously, all at once.

It is admittedly rather difficult to intellectually visualizing how the Supreme Being, who exists in timeless eternity, is somehow able to create and to interact with a universe that is completely subject to time. This undoubtedly is the major reason why most contemporary theistic thinkers prefer to conceive God's eternal existence as being everlasting (existing forever in time), rather than as being timeless (existing continuously outside of time). It is much easier to picture God experiencing the sequencing of time into past, present and future (in a manner similar to human beings) than it is to picture God experiencing the entire range of cosmic time simultaneously for all eternity.

Though perhaps easier to mentally entertain, conceiving God's eternal existence to be everlasting does pose problems of its own. For instance, if the Supreme Being forever exists within time, then the finite, changeable characteristic of time would appear to limit and constrain the infinite enduring characteristic of the one divine nature. Moreover, the notion of divine everlastingness requires that past time is infinite, if God is conceived to have existed forever in time. But if the physical universe of matter and energy had a beginning, together with space and time (as largely accepted by theologians and scientists), then time is not infinite, though God is.

To maintain God's everlasting existence in time, prior to the creation of physical time and the birth of the universe, theorists have been forced to introduced the hypothesis of "metaphysical time" or "infinite duration"; that is, a temporal condition that existed prior to physical time. Unfortunately, these terms are largely undefined; for example: "What is metaphysical time and how does it differ from physical time? Did God create metaphysical time as well? If so, then the concept that God is everlasting falls apart and the divine existence becomes timeless instead."

Contemporary philosophers such as Paul Helm in *Eternal God: A Study of God Without Time* (1997) and Katherine Rogers in *Perfect Being Theology* (2002) argue for God's timelessness. Others such as Richard Swinburne in *The Coherence of Theism* (1977), William Lane Craig in "The Tensed vs. Tenseless Theory of Time: A Watershed for the Conception of Divine Eternity" (1998) and J.R. Lucas (b.1929) in *The Future* (1989) strongly argue for God's temporal everlastingness. In Lucas' own words:

> If we are to characterize God at all, we must say that He is personal, and if personal then temporal, and if temporal then in some sense in time, not outside it.

Still other philosophers such as Eleonore Stump and Norman Kretzmann (1928–1998) in "Eternity" (*Journal of Philosophy*; 1981), Brian Leftow in *Time and Eternity* (1991), and Garrett DeWeese in *God and the Nature of Time* (2004) have attempted to combine the idea of divine timelessness with novel concepts of temporality; such as "omnitemporality" (duration), "eternal-temporal simultaneity" (ET) and "typical temporal property" (TTP).

Intellectual attempts to comprehend the Supreme Being's association with time have naturally raised questions concerning God and the future: questions about divine providence (direction), divine foreknowledge (foresight), divine knowledge of future free-activity and divine prophecy. Of these questions, the thorniest dilemma recurrently wrestled with is the problem of divine foreknowledge and the exercise of human freedom. This logical difficulty can be outlined as follows:

1. If God knows everything, then God knows the future.
2. If God knows the future, then God knows how individuals will act beforehand.
3. If God already knows how an individual will act before they act, then human action has been predetermined.
4. If human action has been predetermined, then there is no human free-will choice.
5. Therefore, divine foreknowledge is incompatible with human freedom.
6. Therefore, either God does not know everything or human beings aren't truly free to act.
7. If God does not know everything, then God isn't truly God.
8. Therefore, God does not exist.

The logical contradiction with this line of reasoning, therefore, is that if God has created truly free individuals, then God doesn't exist. The argument that divine foreknowledge is incompatible with human free-will is known as "theological fatalism."

Both the fatalist argument and the logical contradiction posed by divine foreknowledge and human freedom are easily countered by the notion of divine timelessness. If God is timeless, then divine knowledge is not chronologically sequenced into past, present and future. God, therefore, does not *foreknow* anything, but instead knows everything simultaneously in the eternal Now. Numerous philosophers, including Boethius, Anselm and Aquinas have referred to God's timelessness to firmly lay this particular problem to rest.

While God's timelessly eternal existence provides the most

elegant solution to the problem of divine foreknowledge and human freewill, there have also been other reasonably effective and clever solutions offered, for example:

1. God may know free actions in advance due to the possession of a 'middle knowledge' of how free individuals will act in every circumstance.
2. Similarly, if God knows all possibilities of freely choosing from multiple but finite options, preparation could be made in advance for every contingency.
3. God encodes his knowledge of an individual's free actions into all possible free-will choices.
4. God passively observes future free activity occurring in the created universe without altering it, divinely analogous to reading a cosmic book and being able to open it at any historical page (point in time).
5. God's foreknowledge of how an individual will act does not mean that the free-will decision was predetermined (as stated in preposition 3 above); simply that God's perfect knowledge enables Him to predict with certainty what every free-will choice will be.

Though the concept is more intellectually demanding and more difficult to visualize, comprehending God's existence as being timelessly eternal rather than as being temporally everlasting, best acknowledges the awe-inspiring, transcendent nature of the Absolute One: the creator and sustainer of the entire universe in all his wondrous splendor, beauty, majesty, order and life. Concepts of divine temporality tend to be motivated by the understandable human desire to personally connect with God and to emphasize the Creator's loving interaction with temporal creation, particularly human beings. By doing so helps to dispel the conclusion that God is distant, remote and unconcerned; that the Creator is somehow disconnected and 'outside' creation.

Overemphasizing a personal God, however, runs the risk of unduly anthropomorphicizing the divine nature. Though the Supreme Being is in one sense the epitome of human perfection, the divine nature also infinitely transcends the limited human personality. Moreover, when logically recognized that God must be 'one in all' and 'all in one,' then the Creator cannot exist entirely apart from creation and still be the infinite One. We are compelled by our reason to deduce that God must somehow immanently exist within creation, as well as transcendently exist above and beyond creation—while continuing to remain infinite and eternal in nature.

Whatever the conceptual differences between theistic philosophers and theological theorists concerning God and time, it is important to not lose sight of the forest (of God's eternal nature) for the trees (of imperfect human conception). All acknowledgers of God's existence reasonably conclude that the one nature is eternal, without beginning and without end.

## 9.4   The Divine Nature is Omniscient, All-Knowing

The exercise of clear reasoning also indicates that the Supreme Being is omniscient, all-knowing. Since God's entire nature is infinite and eternal, all attributes of that nature must logically be infinite and eternal as well. God's knowledge, wisdom and understanding must therefore be infinite and eternal.

Since the Supreme Being is the one reality who has eternally existed, the divine nature must have always possessed perfect knowledge, since there is nothing inside or outside of God from where to accrue additional knowledge. God cannot possibly 'grow' in wisdom and understanding since the divine nature is already infinite, without limitation.

Nevertheless, it would be incorrect to conceive of God's omniscience as completely static and forever fixed, or to think that God can never acquire any 'new' knowledge. We must keep in mind that 'old' and 'new' are terms that only properly apply to a succession of time. With God's timeless eternal nature, all knowledge is simultaneously forever old and forever new. In other words, all divine knowledge is timeless, ageless, beyond all temporal categories such as old and new.

Divine omniscience has often been misunderstood to mean that God knows absolutely everything. Atheists in particular have used this meaning to argue that if the Supreme Being does not know everything, then God as defined does not exist. A more accurate definition of divine omniscience is that God knows everything that is logically possible for the divine nature to know. God, therefore, does not know how to make a square circle, or how to create a second God, or how to cease existing—since these are all logical contradictions of the divine nature. Logical impossibilities, then, can't be convincingly used to invalidate God's omniscience or to deny his existence.

Some modern theorists have also proposed a distinction between 'total' omniscience and 'inherent' omniscience—God's ability to know everything that is divinely chosen to know and that is logically possible to know. As one example, British physicist and theologian, John Polkinghorne (b.1930), in *Science and Theology* (1998) has suggested that God chooses to limit divine omniscience in order to preserve free-will and human dignity. As previously discussed in connection with theological fatalism, however, it isn't logically necessary for God to limit his all-knowingness (such as divine foreknowledge) in order to preserve free-will.

Still other theorists have chipped away at the necessity of divine omniscience by suggesting that there are specific forms of knowledge that God possesses, such as "propositional knowledge" ('knowing that'); and certain forms of knowledge that God does not possess, such as "experiential knowledge" ('knowing how'), "procedural knowledge" ('knowing how to do') and "personal knowledge" ('knowing from experience').

Defining God's all-knowingness as simply 'propositional omniscience'—only the knowledge of true facts—reduces the divine nature to a kind of deific storage facility. For God to be truly omniscient, all knowledge must necessarily be accessible to the one nature; otherwise human beings would in many areas be more knowledgeable, more omniscient than God. Unnecessarily weakening the definition of omniscience eventually reduces its meaningfulness use as a fundamental attribute of the divine nature.

## 9.5   The Divine Nature is Omnipotent, All-Powerful

"I am the Almighty God; walk with me and be thou perfect." (Gen 17:1) The familiar biblical term, "Almighty God," concisely describes a fourth essential attribute of the one nature and that of course is omnipotence, unlimited power. Similar to the attributes of infinite, eternal and omniscient, the term omnipotence has often been incorrectly understood and poorly defined, thereby fuelling much meaningless and time-consuming debate.

Since there is only one God who is infinite, all power, energy, impulse, force and drive must logically reside within the divine nature. There is nothing inside or outside God that can possibly increase, decrease or limit the power of the Absolute One. Moreover, all power within the one nature is ultimately anchored in and derives from the divine will, God's will-power. God's will, then, is absolutely free and unfettered.

Does omnipotence mean, then, that God is free and able to do absolutely anything? Of course not; as previously pointed out in connection with divine all-knowingness, it is not possible for God to do the impossible. If God could do the impossible, then it's possible and not impossible, thereby creating a logical contradiction. As we have seen, even God does not have the power to make a square circle or a boulder so massive that it is unliftable (the "riddle of the stone"). Nor does God have the power to create a second God or the power to cease to exist.

The Supreme Being, then, does not have the power to cause necessary, self-existent truth or reality (the divine nature, for example) to begin or end. Also, God does not have the power to act contrary to his own perfect nature nor does God have the power to transform into something he is not. If the divine nature is all-loving, then God does not have the power to hate; if the divine nature is all-truthful, then God does not have the power to lie. As succinctly stated by St. Thomas Aquinas: "Nothing which implies contradiction falls under the omnipotence of God" (*Summa Theologica*); and as later reinforced by C.S. Lewis:

> His Omnipotence means power to do all that is intrinsically possible, not to do the intrinsically impossible. You may attribute miracles to him, but not nonsense. There is no limit to his power." (*The Problem of Pain*; 1940)

From what has been indicated, a more accurate and meaningful understanding of the divine attribute of omnipotence is that God has the perfectly free will-power to do absolutely anything that is logically possible to do in accordance with his own divine nature.

Some monotheistic theorists maintain that with cosmic creation certain limitations have been placed on God's omnipotence. The theory is that God does not exercise absolute command and control over the created universe by the total and continual assertion of his all-powerful will. The slightest exercise of human free choice would certainly be impossible if God omnipotently imposed his will over all things and at all times.

The doctrine of "open theism" claims that with creation, God limits his omnipotence by choice. By contrast, "process theology" proposes that divine omnipotence is limited by necessity; creatures have been granted inherent powers that God cannot, even in principle, override. As well, "dipolar theism" postulates that when flowing through creation, the course of divine omnipotence branches into two streams of power: one stream of authoritarian control and a second stream of subdued persuasion.

Such concepts of 'omnipotent constraint' are based, in part, on a rather narrow understanding of power: it must be applied to be real and it is determined by the degree of influence over other things. As expressed by Charles Hartshorne (1897–2000) in *Man's Vision of God* (1964):

> Power is influence, and perfect power is perfect influence ... power must be exercised on something, at least if by power we mean influence, control ... how can power which is resisted be absolute?

Obviously this conception of power does not apply to God's omnipotence. The one nature possesses all power, whether or not that power is applied or potential, in use or at rest. God's omnipotence is also not measured by its influence over others, since prior to cosmic creation there were no 'others,' yet all power was still within the one nature. Moreover, it can be argued that for the divine will to be truly omnipotent, God must be free to will or not. Rather than limiting omnipotence, the freedom to apply or to withhold the divine will can be regarded as a necessary function of omnipotence.

While the Supreme Being is no doubt free to modify the omnipotent will regarding creation, there must obviously remain sufficient willful engagement to hold creation in existence. Without the divine will there can be no universe; it is this omnipotent will that calls the immense galaxies into being, keeps the stars in their shining place and holds the wandering planets in their regular orbits.

In addition to conceiving God's almighty nature in an absolute sense, omnipotence has also been philosophically regarded in a relative or comparative sense as the notion of "maximal power." In this case, an omnipotent being is simply one that has more power—maximal power—than any other being. According to this idea, it is not necessary that the divine nature has the power to do all things in order to be omnipotent, only that the Supreme Being is able to do more things than any other being. Though this watered-down concept of omnipotence may make it easier to avoid some logical paradoxes and thorny questions, it unfortunately reduces the all-powerful, self-existent Absolute One to simply being the toughest god on the cosmic block.

## 9.6  The Divine Nature is Omnipresent, All-Pervasive

A fifth divine attribute that logically flows from the conception of one God is omnipresence, the property of being present everywhere. The divine nature must be all-pervasive; that is, without interruption, perforation, separation or division. If there were to be gaps in the divine nature, then God wouldn't be the only reality; there would be God and something else. Absolute omnipresence includes the property of "ubiquity," being entirely present everywhere at once—totally and simultaneously—not being partially present in various places at different times.

Absolute omnipresence is much easier to envision and comprehend when the Supreme Being is self-existently alone, within the divine nature prior to cosmic creation. Once the universe together with physical space and time is created, then absolute omnipresence conceptually splits into "transcendence": God's presence beyond the created universe, outside of space and time; and "immanence": God's presence within the created universe, inside space and time.

Various philosophies and religious theologies are characterized by the emphasis given to the concept of divine transcendence, to divine immanence or equally to both. The monotheistic religions of Judaism, Christianity and Islam, for example, all insist that God's omnipresence is both transcendent and immanent. Emanationist pantheism, on the other hand, since it regards God as synonymous with the material universe, denies any transcendent omnipresence of God. Mahayana Buddhism and the Vedanta system of Shankara, since they both regard the material universe as "maya," an unreal cosmic illusion, clearly favour the idea of transcendent omnipresence over divine immanence.

God's immanent presence can often be a confusing concept and while there are a variety of ideas, perhaps the best way to comprehend this immanence is to envision that God is infinitely present to all of space at all times. This does not mean, of course, that the one nature has been particulated into tiny bits of God-stuff and dispersed throughout universal space; but rather that the entire, unlimited being of God is present at every point of physical space. God's nature, instead of being present *in* all space is more correctly conceived as being present *to* all space; which is to say that from a transcendent point of view, all space is immanently present before God.[14]

Instead of a total and direct immanent contact of God with the created universe, some conceptions convey a more limited and indirect immanence. In Eastern Orthodox theology, for example, God's immanent presence in the universe is through the activity of divine, hypostatic energies. For St. Thomas Aquinas, God's immanent presence was determined in three ways: (1) by power over all things, (2) by knowledge of all things and (3) by being the ultimate cause of all things. As eloquently stated in *Summa Theologica*: "God is in all things by his power, inasmuch as all things are subject to his power; he is by his presence in all things, inasmuch as all things are bare and open to his eyes; he is in all things by his essence, inasmuch as he is present to all as the cause of their being."

## 9.7 The Divine Nature is Indivisible and Absolutely Simple

In whatever way that omnipresence is explained or conceived, God must logically be everywhere due to the indivisibility of the one nature as well. If the one nature is all there is, then God can't be separated and pulled apart from himself; there are no empty spaces that are not filled with God. Moreover, since the one nature cannot be divided, God has no parts, and is therefore not 'composed'—nor can he be 'decomposed.' Since the Supreme Being is not an infinitely complex assemblage of bits and pieces but is one, indivisibly pure existence throughout, the divine nature in its essence has been theologically described as being "absolutely simple." The indivisibility and simplicity of the one nature logically requires, then, that God be omnipresent as well.

## 9.8 Omnipresence and the Problem of Hell

Regarding divine omnipresence, the theological question naturally arises: "If God is present everywhere, doesn't this mean that he must also exist in hell and therefore associating with evil?" If hell is not acknowledged to exist, then the problem is quickly and easily resolved. If hell is recognized, then there are a number of resolutions to this question, mostly dependent on how "hell" is defined.

If hell is conceived to be an actual location or condition somewhere within the created universe, then it must be temporal and finite, having no self-existent reality. As such, hell cannot be eternal or infinite. Therefore, applying what has been previously explained concerning immanence, God is present *to* it, not *in* it; or rather, hell is immediately present before God's infinite and eternal nature. Moreover, further applying Aquinas' three understandings of immanence, God is present in hell by his power over it, by his knowledge of it and by his being the cause of its continuing existence. The logical conclusion that God's omnipresence must somehow include hell is clearly stated in biblical scripture: "Whither shall I go from thy Spirit? Or whither shall I flee from thy presence? If I ascend to heaven, thou art there! If I make my bed in Sheol [Hell], thou art there!" (Psalm 139: 7,8)

If hell is conceived as a place or condition of torment for the wicked, then the continuing application of divine justice and retribution can be unsympathetically used to maintain God's necessary presence in hell. A more compassionate resolution is to regard the sufferings of wicked souls as torment *by* their evil actions, rather than punishment *for* their wicked ways. Instead of being banished to hell by God's wrath (a contradiction to the all-loving nature), hell can be regarded as a condition of self-exile by a soul that freely chooses to hate God.

For such a soul, the supernatural awareness of God's perfect being may be experienced as an intense burning light of perfect truth which nakedly reveals the inner iniquity that the wicked soul seeks to hide. Once again, as the Psalmist has written:

> If I say, 'Let only darkness cover me, and the light about me be night, even the darkness is not dark to thee, the night is bright as the day; for darkness is as light with thee." (Psalm 139: 11,12)

And in the Gospel of John, Christ-Jesus similarly stated:

> And this is the judgment, that the light has come into the world, and men loved darkness rather than light, because their deeds were evil. For every one who does evil hates the light, and does not come to the light, lest his deeds should be exposed. But he who does what is true comes to the light, that it may be clearly seen that his deeds have been wrought in God. (Jn 3: 19–21)

While God's omnipresence transcends space and time, such that the self-existent, eternal and infinite nature is present to all space equally, this does not necessarily prevent God from manifesting at a specific place and at a specific time within cosmic creation. These rare and profound appearances are termed, "theophanies." Though theophanic events occur within finite material conditions, they can logically cause no diminution, restriction or compromise of the divine nature.

Instances of theophanic appearances that are well-known in Western monotheism are the voice of the great "I AM" to Moses from the burning bush, the descent of the Holy Spirit as "tongues of fire" at Pentecost, the incarnation of the divine Son in Christ-Jesus and the "real presence" of Christ-Jesus transubstantiated in the sacramental bread and wine of Holy Communion.

One analogous way to conceptualize how the divine nature can theophanically enter time and space and yet still remain unaffected and entirely omnipresent is to imagine a beam of sunlight reflected in a single dewdrop. Even though the beam of light is directly connected to the sun when it touches the dewdrop at a particular point in space and time—reflecting within the dewdrop as a miniature sun—the full glory of the sun continues to remain on high.

## 9.9   The Divine Nature is Changeless and Immutable

An eighth fundamental and logically deduced attribute of the one God is immutability; that is, the divine nature in essence cannot and does not change. If God is all there is, and is eternally so, then the divine nature cannot be added to or subtracted from; it is already complete in every way. Therefore, the divine nature does not grow in wisdom, power, consciousness, being or additional experience. There is nothing inside or outside of the one nature that can possibly alter or change it in any way.

St. Thomas Aquinas in *Summa Theologica* expounded three basic arguments to support divine immutability, which he based on three divine attributes: (1) actuality (real existence), (2) simplicity and (3) perfection. According to Aquinas, God's "aseity," or self-determined existence, is fully actualized; the divine nature is completely realized and all that it can ever be. In other words, God has no need or possibility to become more than he already and actually is. While God certainly has the potential to create and to actualize finite things, the divine nature has no potential for change and hence is immutable.

Regarding Aquinas' argument based on God's absolute simplicity, since the divine nature is an indivisible unity and not a composition of separate parts, if God were to essentially change then everything would have to change together; thereby transforming God into an entirely new being and becoming something he was not. This would not be a minor, insignificant change; but the annihilation of all that God is. Since self-annihilation is something that is logically impossible for God to do, the divine nature cannot possibly change and therefore must be immutable.

The third of Aquinas' arguments for divine unchangeability develops from God's absolutely perfect nature. Since God is all there is and all that can possibly ever exist, there is nothing that can be added to increase the one nature in any way. Philosophically speaking, God is "maximally great" in every possible respect. Since the one nature cannot be improved upon in any way, it is already the best and greatest there is and must continue to be so. Perfection, then, is obviously a further necessary attribute of God's nature. Since God cannot improve or become more complete, his divine nature is not subject to change and is therefore immutable. If God's essential nature could change, then that would indicate a lack or imperfection, which is an unacceptable, logical contradiction.

In connection with God's unchangeable nature, it is important to acknowledge that immutability does not equate to immobility or inactivity; that God is entirely inert and unable to move or act in any way. While movement and activity usually indicate change, and change usually occurs in time, any movement or activity on the part of God must obviously be of a higher order which does not fundamentally alter the immutable divine nature. While God obviously acts and freely expresses his will in such instances as the creation and continuance of the universe, instances of divine movement and activity are analogous to the surface waves of the ocean whose movement does not fundamentally alter the aqueous nature of the ocean itself.

Moreover, even though God is rationally required to be changeless in his essential and fundamental being, this does not mean that the divine consciousness is unable to perceive change or is unaware of change. The mind of God may be aware of changes occurring in time, not as a chronological succession of events, but simultaneously in eternity. Surely, as the creator of the universe and the author of physical time, God must have knowledge of temporal events, even though the divine nature logically remains timeless and enduring, unaffected by the vicissitudes of chronological change.

## 9.10    All the Divine Attributes Apply to Each Other

From the several divine attributes that have been discussed thus far: infinite, eternal, omniscient, omnipotent, omnipresent, ubiquitous, indivisible, simple, perfect, fully actualized and immutable—it is clear that even though the one nature of God transcends the circumscribing activity of the finite human mind, a great deal can be "known with certainty by the natural light of reason" and the power of logic. There are many other attributes of God that could similarly be reasoned, such as unity, veracity, holiness, benignity, necessity (non-contingency) and relatability. Further discussion along these lines, however, is not deemed to be necessary for the purpose of this chapter; which is to present a basic (not a complete) understanding of the divine nature of the one God using the intellectual powers of reason and logic.[15]

Moreover, as precisely expressed in Catholic dogma: "The Divine Attributes are really identical among themselves and with the Divine Essence [God's Nature]." All attributes of God, then, are eternal, infinite, immutable, perfect, and so on. While it may be intellectually helpful to separate and distinguish various attributes, it is important to remember that the divine nature is essentially one, a perfect unity.

# CONCLUSION

THE OBVIOUS, logical conclusion to critically examining the five fundamental arguments of *From Believing to Knowing* is that God certainly exists. Moreover, the "God-hypothesis" is easily concluded to be a far more rational and convincing explanation of life (particularly human life) than the irrational "multiverse theory" or the fatally-flawed "macro-evolutionary theory" of natural science.

Furthermore, one cannot avoid concluding that becoming a well-educated scientist today does not automatically result in the acquisition of sound intellectual reasoning. Well-known scientists such as Richard Dawkins make the most glaring errors in basic logic that even a beginning student in philosophy would avoid.

It is also a sad conclusion of modern life that so few people today (not just scientists) take the time and effort to acquire the intellectual certainty of God's existence. Nevertheless, as the depressingly-negative consequences of the inadequate scientific world-view become more deeply and personally experienced, then more and more desperate thinkers will seriously turn to the God-hypothesis for intellectual solace and certainty.

# NOTES

## CHAPTER 1

1. "Cosmogony" is the astrophysical study of the origin and evolution of the universe. "Cosmology," though similar, is the astrophysical study of the history, structure and constituent dynamics of the universe.

2. Establishing the singular beginning of the universe is not solely dependent on the expansion velocity of galaxies. Supporting evidence has also been obtained from the burning of stars, the ages of the oldest stars, the deterioration of radiometric elements (uranium and thorium, for example) and the equations of general relativity.

3. The "multiverse" or "meta-universe" is the hypothetical sum of manifold, diverse universes including our own that would comprise the entirety of physical reality. "Parallel universes" refers to different hypothetical universes within the multiverse that create their own time and space and which, therefore, would not affect each other, but would instead share a parallel existence.

4. "So why do we need a quantum theory of gravity? A strong, but nevertheless often nebulous, desire to

present a unified theoretical framework at the level of fundamental physics populates the folklore of physicists and often fuels the search for a quantum theory of gravity. Arguments to this effect, relying—if made explicit at all—on metaphysical considerations, typically elicit some principles of unity of nature or of scientific method." (Christian Wuthrich; *To Quantize or Not to Quantize: Fact and Folklore in Quantum Gravity*, 2005)

## CHAPTER 2

5. This developmental condition, of course, applied to mankind in general. From earliest times, there have also been a select few individuals, initiates, who have accelerated the regular course of human evolution, advancing their knowledge and abilities beyond ordinary development.

## CHAPTER 3

6. A black hole singularity is a region of space within the observable universe where the central gravitational force is so strong that visible light is unable to escape and, hence, appears as a "black hole." General relativity describes a black hole as a region of empty space with a point-like singularity at the center and an event horizon at the outer edge, a surface in space-time that marks a point of no return.

7. As stated by German scientist, Karl Vogt (1817–1895): "The brain secretes thought as the stomach secretes gastric juice, the liver bile, and the kidneys urine."

8. Current brain researchers are forced to perform exotic conceptual gymnastics to empirically explain human

consciousness and self-awareness. According to contemporary American philosopher, Hud Hudson, human beings are cerebral, multiple-located, four-dimensional space-time worms:

> Human persons ... Are most often found somewhere within the lifespan and somewhere beneath the skin of a living human organism. Presumably, then, they are those (spatially and temporally gappy) space time worms that are certain proper temporal parts of the brain and the central nervous system of living human organisms. (*A Materialist Metaphysics of the Human Person*; 2001)

To neuroscientist, Joseph LeDoux (b.1949), the human self was not contained within the grey matter of the brain either but, similar to Hudson, existed in the spaces between brain cells:

> 'You are your synapses.' Synapses are the spaces between brain cells, but are much more. They are the channels of communication between brain cells, and the means by which most of what the brain does is accomplished. (*Synaptic Self*; 2002)

## CHAPTER 6

9.   "Creationism," in the broad sense of the term, refers to the religious belief that the universe and everything in it: mankind, life, plants, animals, stars and planets—has been created in their original form by God. Since the 1980s, however, the term has become specifically associated with Christian fundamentalist opposition (particularly in the USA) to modern evolutionary theory and the promotion of a literal interpretation of the seven days of creation in Genesis as actual 24-hour time

periods. Not only the general scientific community, but also many mainstream Christian denominations such as Anglicans, Lutherans and Roman Catholics reject the literal creationist version of cosmogenetic events.

## CHAPTER 7

10. "Naturalism" is a system of philosophical thought which alleges that all observable phenomena can be explained in terms of natural causes and natural laws.
11. The source of these syllogistic summaries was an internet article by J.P. Moreland, "Does the Argument from Mind Provide Evidence for God?"

## CHAPTER 8

12. "Mirror neurons" are a distinct class of neurons that have been discovered in the ventral, premotor cortex of the macaque monkey. These neurons fire when the monkey itself acts or observes the same action in another monkey (or human). The neuron, then, is capable of 'mirroring' the behaviour of another. These neurons have not as yet been directly observed in humans, but similar behaviour is currently suggestive.

## CHAPTER 9

13. Surprising to many, it is a dogma of the Catholic Church that "God can be known with intellectual certainty." According to the *Catechism of the Catholic Church*:

> Created in God's image and called to know and love him, the person who seeks God discovers certain

ways of coming to know him. These are also called proofs for the existence of God, not in the sense of proofs in the natural sciences, but rather in the sense of "converging and convincing arguments," which allow us to attain certainty about the truth. These "ways" of approaching God from creation have a twofold point of departure: the physical world, and the human person. (paragraph 31)

Our holy mother, the Church, holds and teaches that God, the first principle and last end of all things, can be known with certainty from the created world by the natural light of human reason. (paragraph 36)

14. The internet article, "The Omnipresence of God," by Allan Turner was very helpful in this area.

15. The First Vatican Council (1868) provided a comprehensive and concise summary of the divine attributes:

The Holy, Catholic, Apostolic and Roman Church believes and acknowledges that there is one true and living God, Creator and Lord of Heaven and earth, almighty, eternal, immeasurable, incomprehensible, infinite in will, understanding and every perfection. Since He is one, singular, completely simple and unchangeable spiritual substance, He must be declared to be in reality and in essence, distinct from the world, supremely happy in Himself and from Himself, and inexpressibly loftier than anything besides Himself which either exists or can be imagined.

# SELECT BIBLIOGRAPHY

(in alphabetical order)

- C.S. Lewis, *Mere Christianity* (HarperCollins, 2009)

- C.S. Lewis, *The Case for Christianity* (Simon & Schuster, 1996)

- Immanuel Kant, *Critique of Pure Reason* (Hackett Publishing Company Ltd., 1996)

- James Jeans, *The Mysterious Universe* (Kessinger Publishing, 2011)

- Murdo MacDonald-Bayne, *Divine Healing of Mind and Body* (C.W. Daniel, 2004)

- Richard Dawkins, *The God Delusion* (Houghton Mifflin Harcourt, 2008)

- Rudolf Steiner, *An Outline of Occult Science* (Rudolf Steiner Press, 2011)

- Saint Thomas Aquinas, *Summa Theologica* (Library of Alexandria, 1952)

- Stephen Hawking, *A Brief History of Time* (Bantam Books, 1998)

- The Three Initiates, *The Kybalion: A Study of the Hermetic Philosophy of Ancient Egypt and Greece* (Murine Press, 2007)

- Yogi Ramacharaka, *Advanced Course in Yogi Philosophy and Oriental Occultism* (Cosimo Inc., 2007)

- Yogi Ramacharaka, *Raja Yoga or Mental Development* (Indo-European Publishing, 2007)

Made in the USA
Columbia, SC
07 September 2017